CEH™ v9
Certified Ethical Hacker
Version 9 Practice Tests

Raymond Blockmon

SYBEX®
A Wiley Brand

Executive Editor: Jim Minatel
Development Editor: Kim Wimpsett
Technical Editors: Dwayne Machinski; Paul Calatayud; Charles Tendell
Production Editor: Dassi Zeidel
Copy Editor: Judy Flynn
Editorial Manager: Mary Beth Wakefield
Production Manager: Kathleen Wisor
Supervising Producer: Rich Graves
Book Designers: Judy Fung and Bill Gibson
Proofreader: Nancy Carrasco
Indexer: Ted Laux
Project Coordinator, Cover: Brent Savage
Cover Designer: Wiley
Cover Image: © Getty Images Inc./Jeremy Woodhouse

Copyright © 2016 by John Wiley & Sons, Inc., Indianapolis, Indiana

Published simultaneously in Canada

ISBN: 978-1-119-25215-3

ISBN: 978-1-119-29516-7 (ebk.)

ISBN: 978-1-119-25216-0 (ebk.)

Manufactured in the United States of America

For general information on our other products and services or to obtain technical support, please contact our Customer Care Department within the U.S. at (877) 762-2974, outside the U.S. at (317) 572-3993 or fax (317) 572-4002.

Wiley publishes in a variety of print and electronic formats and by print-on-demand. Some material included with standard print versions of this book may not be included in e-books or in print-on-demand. If this book refers to media such as a CD or DVD that is not included in the version you purchased, you may download this material at http://booksupport.wiley.com. For more information about Wiley products, visit www.wiley.com.

Library of Congress Control Number: 2016934920

I'd like to dedicate this exam book to my children, Samarea, Raeleah, Ray J, and Savion. These four are the inspiration in all that I do.

I would also like to dedicate this to my mom, Olga Blockmon, and my dad, Paul Blockmon. They have been there for me at every step of the way. My father is truly the inspiration of what I wanted to be—a hard worker and a dedicated family man. He epitomizes what a father should truly be. My mother always believed in me and always spared no expense when it came to supporting me. Thank you, Mom and Dad, for everything. There is no way I can ever repay you.

And to my Lord and Savior Jesus Christ—with You, nothing can stop me.

Acknowledgments

Thank you to Dan Kasperon, the chief building inspector of Suisun City, California. This gentleman gave me a chance to do something great. He hired me as an intern for desktop support. Little did I know, I was the only person in the IT shop. I supported over 300 employees, and at several different locations. Needless to say, it was the best job I have ever had in my life; great people and a great city to work for.

Thank you to Dwayne Machinski and John Glover—two of the best IT pros I have ever had the pleasure of working with. They gave me the tools and confidence to tackle anything—and they believed in me. Thanks guys.

Thank you to Jim Minatel and the Wiley & Son's publishing family for giving me the opportunity to work on this wonderful project. I truly thank each and every one of you.

About the Author

Raymond Blockmon worked as an intern for the Suisun City, California, government offices. California. Supporting more than 300 personnel and several locations, he realized that this was a job he enjoyed. Eventually, he would move on and enlist in the army as a fire direction specialist.

Raymond served two combat tours in Iraq as a fire support specialist and a fire support officer. He received his commission as a field artillery officer at Cameron University, Lawton, Oklahoma. He later transitioned as a signal officer. Raymond was then assigned as the regional network operation security center officer in charge at Camp Arifjan, Kuwait. He directly oversaw all US Army installation tier 2 network operations in the Middle East, to include Egypt, Saudi Arabia, Iraq, Bahrain, Jordan, and Qatar.

He was then selected to become a cyber network defense manager with the newly activated US Army Cyber Protection Brigade at Fort Gordon, Georgia.

Raymond has also taught CEH, CISSP, and PMP courses and freelances as a CISSP and PMP course developer for commercial vendors.

Raymond holds a bachelor of science degree in Computer Information Systems from Cameron University and a master of arts in Organizational Leadership from Brandman University. His certifications are Network+, CCNA Routing and Switching, CEH, CISSP, and PMP. Raymond is currently enrolled at Webster University and is pursuing a master of arts in Information Technology Management.

Contents

Introduction

This exam book is designed to give the CEH candidate a realistic idea of what the CEH exam will look like. As a candidate, you should be familiar with Wireshark, Nmap, and other tools. To get the most out of these exams, you should consider constructing a virtual lab and practicing with the tools to become familiar with viewing the logs that are generated. In preparing for the CEH exam, you will benefit greatly by using YouTube. YouTube is a goldmine of information—and it's free. It is also recommended that you keep up with the latest malware and cybersecurity news provided online. Most cybersecurity-related websites provide insight on the latest vulnerabilities and exploits that are in the wild. Keeping up to date with this information will only add value to your CEH knowledge and will help solidify your understanding even more.

Finally, this exam book should not be the only resource you use to prepare. You should use other exam books and study guides as well. The more diverse the exposure in terms of reading and preparation material, the better. Take your time studying; invest at least one hour per day prior to your exam date.

If you have not already read *CEHv9: Certified Ethical Hacker Version 9 Study Guide* by Sean-Philip Oriyano (Sybex, 2016) and you're not seeing passing grades on these practice tests, you should invest in the Study Guide since it is an excellent resource to master any of the CEH topics that may be causing you problems.

Chapter

1

Practice Test 1

1. Which of the following is considered a passive reconnaissance action?
   - **A.** Searching through the local paper
   - **B.** Calling Human Resources
   - **C.** Using the `nmap -sT` command
   - **D.** Conducting a man-in-the-middle attack
   - **E.** Setting up a rogue hot spot

2. Which encryption was selected by NIST as the principal method for providing confidentiality after the DES algorithm?
   - **A.** 3DES
   - **B.** Twofish
   - **C.** RC4
   - **D.** AES

3. What tool is able to conduct a man-in-the-Middle Attack on an 802.3 environment?
   - **A.** Ettercap
   - **B.** Cain & Abel
   - **C.** Wireshark
   - **D.** Nmap

4. What is the difference between a traditional firewall and an IPS?
   - **A.** Firewalls do not generate logs.
   - **B.** IPS cannot drop packets.
   - **C.** IPS does not follow rules.
   - **D.** IPS can dissect packets.

5. Why is it important to scan your target network slowly?
   - **A.** To avoid alerting the IDS
   - **B.** It is not necessary to scan the network slowly.
   - **C.** To evade the firewall
   - **D.** Services may not have started, so starting slowly ensures that you capture services that started late.

6. You are the senior manager in the IT department for your company. What is the most cost effective way to prevent social engineering attacks?
   - **A.** Install HIDS.
   - **B.** Ensure that all patches are up-to-date.
   - **C.** Monitor and control all email activity.
   - **D.** Implement user awareness training.

7. In which phase within the ethical hacking framework do you alter or delete log information?
   - **A.** Scanning and enumeration
   - **B.** Gaining access

   C. Reconnaissance

   D. Covering tracks

8. A hacker is conducting the following on the target workstation: `nmap -sT 192.33.10.5`. The attacker is in which phase?

   A. Covering tracks

   B. Enumeration

   C. Scanning and enumeration

   D. Gaining access

9. Which encryption algorithm is a symmetric stream cipher?

   A. AES

   B. ECC

   C. RC4

   D. PGP

10. What is the most important aspect when conducting a penetration test?

   A. Receiving a formal written agreement

   B. Documenting all actions and activities

   C. Remediating serious threats immediately

   D. Maintaining proper handoff with the information assurance team

11. You are a CISO for a giant tech company. You are charged with implementing an encryption cipher for your new mobile devices that will be introduced in 2017. What encryption standard will you most likely choose?

   A. RC4

   B. MD5

   C. ECC

   D. Skipjack

12. What does a SYN scan accomplish?

   A. It establishes a full TCP connection.

   B. It establishes only a "half open" connection.

   C. It opens an ACK connection with the target.

   D. It detects all closed ports on a target system.

13. What is the major vulnerability for an ARP request?

   A. It sends out an address request to all the hosts on the LAN.

   B. The address is returned with a username and password in cleartext.

   C. The address request can cause a DoS.

   D. The address request can be spoofed with the attacker's MAC address.

14. You are the CISO for a popular social website. You recently learned that your web servers have been compromised with the SSL Heart Bleed zero day exploit. What will be your most likely first course of action to defend against?

    A. Patch all systems.

    B. Establish new cryptographic keys.

    C. Shut down Internet-facing web services.

    D. Restrict access to sensitive information.

15. In what phase is an attacker who is currently conducting a successful man-in-the-middle attack?

    A. Gaining access

    B. Maintaining access

    C. Reconnaissance

    D. Covering tracks

16. What method of exploitation allows the adversary to test for SQL queries within the URL?

    A. SQL injection

    B. XSS

    C. Spear phishing

    D. Ruby on Rails injection method

17. What is the default TTL values for Microsoft Windows 7 OS?

    A. 64

    B. 128

    C. 255

    D. 256

18. Which input value would you utilize in order to evaluate and test for SQL injection vulnerabilities?

    A. SQL test

    B. admin and password

    C. || or |!

    D. 1'or'1'='1

19. What is the downside of using SSH with Telnet when it comes to security?

    A. SSH encrypts the traffic and credentials.

    B. You cannot see what the adversary is doing.

    C. Data is sent in the clear.

    D. You do not know what keys you are using.

20. What year did the Ping of Death first appear?

    A. 1992

    B. 1989

    C. 1990

    D. 1996

21. Which of the following viruses was the most infectious?

    A. The Melisa virus

    B. I Love You Virus

    C. Blue Cross virus punter

    D. Stuxnet

22. You are part of the help desk team. You receive a ticket from one of your users that their computer is periodically slow. The user also states that from time to time, documents have either disappeared or have been moved from their original location to another. You remote desktop to the user's computer and investigate. Where is the most likely place to see if any new processes have started?

    A. The Processes tab in Task Manager

    B. `C:\Temp`

    C. The Logs tab in Task Manager

    D. `C:\Windows\System32\User`

23. As a network engineer, you received the task of bridging two corporate facilities by way of wireless communication. These facilities are more than 20 miles apart, contain more than 400 employees at each site, and have a $20,000 budget. Each site has a single-mode fiber connection. Which antenna would you use to bridge the gap?

    A. Multimode fiber

    B. Very small aperture terminal (VSAT)

    C. Omni direction antenna

    D. Directional antenna

24. What does a checksum indicate?

    A. That the data has made it to its destination

    B. That the three-way TCP/IP handshake finished

    C. That there were changes to the data during transit or at rest

    D. The size of the data after storage

25. Out of the following, which is one of RSA's registered key strengths?

    A. 1,024 bits

    B. 256 bits

    C. 128 bits

    D. 512 bits

26. To provide nonrepudiation for email, which algorithm would you choose to implement?

    A. AES

    B. DSA

   C. 3DES

   D. Skipjack

27. Which of the following describes a race condition?

   A. Where two conditions occur at the same time and there is a chance that arbitrary commands can be executed with a user's elevated permissions, which can then be used by the adversary

   B. Where two conditions cancel one another out and arbitrary commands can be used based on the user privilege level

   C. Where two conditions are executed under the same user account

   D. Where two conditions are executed simultaneously with elevated user privileges

28. Your end clients report that they cannot reach any website on the external network. As the network administrator, you decide to conduct some fact finding. Upon your investigation, you determine that you are able to ping outside of the LAN to external websites using their IP address. Pinging websites with their domain name resolution does not work. What is most likely causing the issue?

   A. The firewall is blocking DNS resolution.

   B. The DNS server is not functioning correctly.

   C. The external websites are not responding.

   D. HTTP GET request is being dropped at the firewall from going out.

29. You are the security administration for your local city. You just installed a new IPS. Other than plugging it in and applying some basic IPS rules, no other configuration has been made. You come in the next morning and you discover that there was a so much activity generated by the IPS in the logs that it is too time consuming to view. What most likely caused the huge influx of logs from the IPS?

   A. The clipping level was established.

   B. There was a DoS attack on the network.

   C. The LAN experienced a switching loop.

   D. There was no baseline established.

30. Which method would be considered a client-side attack?

   A. Cross-site scripting (XSS)

   B. Man-in-the-middle attack

   C. Watering hole attack

   D. Denial of service (DoS)

31. As a penetration tester, only you and a few key selected individuals from the company will know of the targeted network that will be tested. You also have zero knowledge of your target other than the name and location of the company. What type of assessment is this called?

   A. Gray box testing

   B. White box testing

C. Black box testing

D. Blue box testing

32. As an attacker, you found your target. You spend the next two weeks observing and watching personnel move in and move out of the facility. You also observe how the front desk handles large packages that are delivered as well as people who do not have access badges. You finally come up with a solid schedule of security patrols that you see being conducted. What is it that you are doing?

A. Casing the target

B. Gaining access

C. Maintaining access

D. Reconnaissance

33. Which scanning tool is more likely going to yield accurate results for the hacker?

A. Ncat

B. Nmap

C. Ping

D. Nslookup

34. Why would an attacker conduct an open TCP connection scan using Ncat?

A. The attacker does not want to attack the system.

B. The attacker made a mistake using the nmap function.

C. The attacker is trying to connect to network services.

D. The attacker is trying to see what ports are open for connection.

35. Why would an attacker want to avoid tapping into a fiber-optic line?

A. It costs a lot of money to tap into a fiber line.

B. If done wrong, it could cause the entire connection signal to drop, therefore bringing unwanted attention from the targeted organization.

C. The network traffic would slow down significantly.

D. Tapping the line could alert an IPS/IDS.

36. You are an attacker who has successfully infiltrated your target's web server. You performed a web defacement on the targeted organization's website, and you were able to create your own credential with administrative privileges. Before conducting data exfiltration, what is the next move?

A. Log in to the new user account that you created.

B. Go back and delete or edit the logs.

C. Ensure that you log out of the session.

D. Ensure that you migrate to a different session and log out.

37. What is the main drawback to using Kerberos?

    A.   Symmetric keys can be compromised if not secured.

    B.   Kerberos uses weak cryptography and keys can be easily cracked.

    C.   Kerberos uses asymmetric cryptography and can be easily exploited.

    D.   The adversary can replay the ticket-granting ticket to gain access to a system or service.

38. Where is the password file located on a Windows system?

    A.   `C:\Windows\temp`

    B.   `C:\Win\system\config`

    C.   `C:\Windows\accounts\config`

    D.   `C:\Windows\system32\config`

39. Which response would the adversary receive on closed ports if they conducted an XMAS scan?

    A.   RST

    B.   RST/ACK

    C.   No Response

    D.   FIN/ACK

40. Why would the adversary encode their payload before sending it to the target victim?

    A.   Encoding the payload will not provide any additional benefit.

    B.   By encoding the payload, the adversary actually encrypts the payload.

    C.   The encoded payload can bypass the firewall because there is no port associated with the payload.

    D.   Encoding the payload can bypass IPS/IDS detection because it changes the signature.

41. Which password is more secure?

    A.   !9Apple

    B.   pass123!!

    C.   P@$$w0rD

    D.   keepyourpasswordsecuretoyourself

42. Which of the following best describes DNS poisoning?

    A.   The adversary intercepts and replaces the victims MAC address with their own.

    B.   The adversary replaces their malicious IP address with the victim's IP address for the domain name.

    C.   The adversary replaces the legitimate domain name with the malicious domain name.

    D.   The adversary replaces the legitimate IP address that is mapped to the domain name with the malicious IP address.

43. Which of the following allows the adversary to forge certificates for authentication?

A. Wireshark

B. Ettercap

C. Cain & Abel

D. Ncat

44. Which encryption standard is used in WEP?

A. AES

B. RC5

C. MD5

D. RC4

45. You are sitting inside of your office and you notice a strange person in the parking lot with what appears to be a tall antenna connected to a laptop. What is the stranger most likely doing?

A. Brute-forcing their personal electronic device

B. Wardriving

C. Warflying

D. Bluesnarfing

46. As a network administrator, you see a familiar IP address pinging the broadcast address. What do you believe is happening?

A. Smurf attack

B. DNS poisoning

C. Man-in-the-middle attack

D. Trojan virus infecting the gateway

47. Which best describes a denial of service (DoS)?

A. Victim's computer is infected with a virus.

B. A misconfigured switch is in a switching loop.

C. An adversary is forging a certificate.

D. An adversary is consuming all available memory of a target system by opening as many "half-open" connections on a web server as possible.

48. In the Windows SAM file, what attributes would indicate to the adversary that a given account is an administrator account?

A. 500

B. 1001

C. ADM

D. ADMIN_500

49. Which regional Internet registry is responsible for North and South America?

  A. RIPE

  B. AMERNIC

  C. LACNIC

  D. ARIN

50. Which of following actions is the last step in scanning a target?

  A. Scan for vulnerabilities.

  B. Identify live systems.

  C. Discover open ports.

  D. Identify the OS and servers.

51. Which of the following best describes the ICMP Type 8 code?

  A. Device is being filtered

  B. Network route is incorrect or missing

  C. Echo request

  D. Destination unreachable

52. Which of the following options shows the well-known ports?

  A. 0 to 1023

  B. 0 to 255

  C. 1024 to 49151

  D. 1 to 128

53. What is war dialing?

  A. An adversary conducting a DoS on a modem

  B. An adversary dialing to see what modems are open

  C. An adversary using a modem as an evil twin

  D. An adversary verifying closed modems

54. Which of the following switches for the Nmap command fingerprints an operating system?

  A. -sO

  B. -sFRU

  C. -sA

  D. -sX

55. What command would the adversary use to show all the systems within the domain using the command line interface in Windows?

  A. `netstat -R /domain`

  B. `net view /<domain_name>:domain`

  C. `net view /domain:<domain_name>`

  D. `netstat /domain:<domain_name>`

56. You are a passenger in an airport terminal. You glance across the terminal and notice a man peering over the shoulder over a young woman as she uses her tablet. What do you think he is doing?

  A. Wardriving

  B. Shoulder surfing

  C. War shouldering

  D. Shoulder jacking

57. You are the attacker that has successfully conducted a SQL injection vulnerability assessment on a target site. Which keyword would you use to join the target database with your own malicious database as part of the SQL injection?

  A. UNION

  B. ADD

  C. SELECT

  D. JOIN

58. Which option describes the concept of injecting code into a portion of data in memory that allows for abritary commands to be executed?

  A. Buffer overflow

  B. Crash

  C. Memory overflow

  D. Data overflow

59. Of the following methods, which one acts as a middleman between an external network and the private network by initiating and establishing the connection?

  A. Proxy server

  B. Firewall

  C. Router

  D. Switch

60. As an attacker, you successfully exploited your target using a service that should have been disabled. The service had vulnerabilities that you were able to exploit with ease. What may be the issue here?

  A. The administrator did not apply the correct patches.

  B. The web server was improperly configured.

  C. You are dealing with a honeypot.

  D. The firewall was not configured correctly.

61. Where is the logfile that is associated with the a activities of the last user that signed in within a Linux system?

  A. /var/log/user_log

  B. /var/log/messages

  C. /var/log/lastlog

  D. /var/log/last_user

62. What default port does SSH utilize?

   A. Port 22

   B. Port 21

   C. Port 443

   D. Port 25

63. As a pentester, you are hired to conduct an assessment on a group of systems for your client. You are provided with a list of critical assets, a list of domain controllers, and a list of virtual share drives. Nothing else was provided. What type of test are you conducting?

   A. White hat testing

   B. Gray hat testing

   C. Gray box testing

   D. Red hat testing

64. Which of the following best describes what is meant by the term *firewalking*?

   A. Decrementing the TTL value by 1 past the firewall will show if a port is opened.

   B. Causing a denial of service on the firewall with a ping flood

   C. Conducting a ping sweep on the firewall

   D. Setting the TTL passed the router to determine what servers and other hosts are available

65. Which tool can be used to conduct layer 3 scanning and enumeration?

   A. Cain & Abel

   B. John the ripper

   C. Ping-eater

   D. Nmap

66. What port number or numbers is/are associated with the IP protocol?

   A. 0 to 65535

   B. No ports

   C. 53

   D. 80

67. Which two protocols are connectionless?

   A. IP and TCP

   B. IP and FTP

   C. IP and UDP

   D. TCP and UDP

68. What is the role of an individual who interrogates a system with permission?

   A. White hat

   B. Gray hat

    C. Black hat

    D. Red hat

69. What is patch management?

    A. Deploying patches when they are available

    B. Testing patches in a testing environment before they are deployed to the production environment

    C. Deploying patches at the end of the month

    D. Determining what vulnerabilities are currently on your network and deploying patches immediately to eliminate the threat

70. At which layer of the OSI model does FTP reside?

    A. Session

    B. Application

    C. Network

    D. Transport

71. Which exploitation was associated with the heart bleed attack?

    A. Buffer overflow

    B. Man in the middle

    C. Fraggle attack

    D. Smurf attack

72. Which switch in Nmap invokes the XMAS scan?

    A. -sX

    B. -sS

    C. -xS

    D. -sT

73. Which of the following best describes a fingerprint scan?

    A. Scanning for vulnerabilities

    B. Using the -sX switch for Nmap

    C. Matching characteristics from a scan to a database in Nmap

    D. Check to see what ports are open by firewalking

74. Which option describes a client-side attack targeting web applications?

    A. SQL injection

    B. Cross-site malware injection

    C. Cross-site scripting

    D. SQL site scripting

75. What port is used by DNS?

  A. 80

  B. 8080

  C. 53

  D. 25

76. In Linux, what file allows you to see user information such as full name, phone number, and office information?

  A. shadow file

  B. passwd file

  C. userinfo file

  D. useraccount file

77. In a packet analyzer, where can you see where the FIN flag is set?

  A. TCP – Header

  B. TCP – Packet

  C. UDP – Flags

  D. TCP – Flags

78. Which type of packet does a fraggle attack use to create a DoS attack?

  A. TCP

  B. IP

  C. ICMP

  D. UDP

79. Which instruction value is used to invoke a NOP (non-operating procedure)?

  A. 0x99

  B. 0x91

  C. 0xGH

  D. 0x90

80. What protocol would you use to conduct banner grabbing?

  A. FTP

  B. IRC

  C. DNS

  D. Telnet

81. Which of the following functions is no longer utilized within IPv6?

  A. Multicast

  B. Anycast

   C. Unicast

   D. Broadcast

82. What are you creating when you set up a server with certain configurations and document step-by-step instructions?

   A. Baseline

   B. Procedure

   C. Technical advisory

   D. Guideline

83. Which application uses two ports?

   A. Telnet

   B. ICMP

   C. HTTPS

   D. FTP

84. Which of the following protocols periodically force the client and server to challenge each other for mutual authentication?

   A. CHAP

   B. POP

   C. PAP

   D. PPE

85. Which of the following is part of the account management life cycle?

   A. Account provisioning

   B. Access Denied

   C. User authentication

   D. None of the above

86. Which of the following activities describes the act of a person rummaging through a trash container looking for sensitive information?

   A. Trash jumping

   B. Dumpster party

   C. Trash diving

   D. Dumpster diving

87. What are two common ports used to connect to a web server?

   A. 80 and 25

   B. 80 and 8080

   C. 443 and 53

   D. 20 and 21

88. When considering the risks of local storage vs. third-party cloud storage, which statement is most accurate?

   A. Cloud storage is more secure because the commercial vendor has trained security professionals.

   B. When storage is local, you are responsible and accountable for the storage services.

   C. You can sue the cloud provider for damages.

   D. The cloud has more layers of security than traditional local storage infrastructures.

89. What would you call an IP address joined with a port number?

   A. TCP/IP

   B. Connection-oriented protocol

   C. TCP/IP socket

   D. Socket

90. A classification label is associated with which of the following?

   A. A subject

   B. A file

   C. An object

   D. A folder

91. Which of the following tools allows you to create certificates that are not officially signed by a CA?

   A. Cain & Abel

   B. Nmap

   C. Ettercap

   D. Darkether

92. Which RAID configuration is not viable or used anymore?

   A. RAID-1

   B. RAID-3

   C. RAID-5

   D. RAID-2

93. This protocol is used for authentication purposes; it sends cleartext usernames and passwords with no forms of encryption or a means of challenging. What authentication protocol is this?

   A. CHAP

   B. POP

   C. PAP

   D. MSCHAP

94. "Something you are" is considered a part of which authentication factor type?

    A. Type 1

    B. Type 3

    C. Type 2

    D. Multifactor authentication

95. When two or more authentication methods are used, it is called?

    A. Multitiered authentication factor

    B. Multifactor authentication

    C. Multicommon factor authentication

    D. Multiauthentication factor

96. Which of the following has no key associated with it?

    A. MD5

    B. AES

    C. Skipjack

    D. PGP

97. Which operating system build provides a suite of tools for network defense purposes?

    A. Kali Linux

    B. Windows Server 2012 R2

    C. FreeBSD

    D. Security Onion

98. Which operating system build provides a suite of tools for network offensive (attack your target) purposes?

    A. Kali Linux

    B. Windows Server 2012 R2

    C. FreeBSD

    D. Security Onion

99. What is a major drawback of antivirus software?

    A. It can be extremely slow.

    B. It must have the latest virus definitions.

    C. It can take up a lot of host resources.

    D. It requires a lot of effort to administer.

100. Which of the following applications would you use to implement an IDS/IPS solution in order to defend your network?

    A. Kali Linux

    B. Windows Vista

C. Ncat

D. Suricata

101. What is the maximum byte size for a UDP packet?

A. 65,535

B. 65,507

C. 1,500

D. 65,527

102. As an attacker, which of the following resources would you start with first to form a foot-print of your target during the reconnaissance phase?

A. Nmap using the –s0 switch

B. Kali Linux

C. The help wanted section in the newspaper

D. Calling the help desk masquerading as an authorized user

103. When sending a packet with a FIN flag set, what will the target respond with if the port is open?

A. RST is returned.

B. No response is returned.

C. RST/ACK is returned.

D. SYN/ACK is returned.

104. What is the result of conducting a MAC flood on a switch?

A. The switch would fail to respond.

B. It would create a DoS.

C. The switch would operate as if it were a hub.

D. The switch would continue to operate as normal.

105. Which of the following is the correct way to search for a specific IP address in Wireshark?

A. `ip.addr = 192.168.1.100`

B. `ip == 192.168.1.100`

C. `ip = 192.168.1.199`

D. `ip.addr == 192.168.1.100`

106. Which of the following is a Type 2 access control method?

A. Fingerprint

B. PIN

C. GPS location

D. Token access card

107. What type of attack best defines the following situation? An email contains a link with the subject line "Congratulations on your cruise!" The email instructs the reader to click a hyperlink to claim the cruise. When the link is clicked, the reader is presented with a series of questions within an online form, such as name, social security number, and date of birth.

A. Email phishing

B. Spear phishing

C. Social engineering

D. Identity theft

108. A network of zombie computers used to execute a DDoS on a target system is called?

A. Botnet

B. Whaling

C. Social engineering

D. DoS

109. Cipher locks, mantraps, and bollards are considered what?

A. Physical controls

B. Technical controls

C. Crime prevention through environmental design

D. Physical barriers

110. Which of the following describes the X.509 standard?

A. It defines the LDAP structure.

B. It is a symmetric encryption algorithm.

C. It uses a sandbox method for security.

D. It describes the standard for creating a digital certificate.

111. Which of the following best describes steganography?

A. A symmetric encryption algorithm

B. Allowing the public to use your private key

C. Hiding information within a picture or concealing it in an audio format

D. Encrypting data using transposition and substitution

112. In which of the following classifications would a honeypot be in most cases?

A. Enticement

B. Entrapment

C. Social engineering

D. Honeynet

113. At what bandwidth does an 802.11a access point operate?

    A. 54 Mbps

    B. 1 Gbps

    C. 5 GHz

    D. 2.4 GHz

114. What is the governing council of the CEH exam?

    A. (ISC)2

    B. EC-Council

    C. CompTIA

    D. Microsoft

115. What Transport layer protocol does DHCP operate with?

    A. IP

    B. TCP

    C. ICMP

    D. UDP

116. According to the diagram, what is the IANA ID?

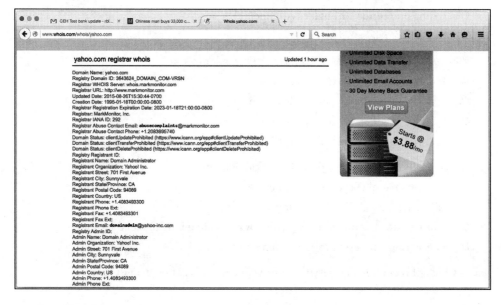

    A. 292

    B. 94089

    C. US

    D. 4083493300

117. According to the following screen shot, what process identification is Terminal running?

```
●  ●  ●                ⌂ rblockmon — top — 80×24
Processes: 188 total, 4 running, 8 stuck, 176 sleeping, 872 threads      18:48:07
Load Avg: 1.96, 1.52, 2.31  CPU usage: 37.77% user, 15.73% sys, 46.48% idle
SharedLibs: 16M resident, 17M data, 0B linkedit.
MemRegions: 30804 total, 1184M resident, 45M private, 431M shared.
PhysMem: 4076M used (950M wired), 19M unused.
VM: 454G vsize, 1064M framework vsize, 0(0) swapins, 0(0) swapouts.
Networks: packets: 633227/753M in, 385518/53M out.
Disks: 70433/2394M read, 121601/3290M written.

PID   COMMAND      %CPU  TIME       #TH  #WQ  #PORT MEM     PURG  CMPRS   PGRP PPID
718   firefox      96.1  34:22.42   87/4  3   517+  720M-  4096B  197M+   718  1
861   plugin-conta 60.7  01:33.63   50/1  2   441+  342M+  0B     26M+    718  718
0     kernel_task  21.5  07:45.74   92/4  0   2     348M-  0B     0B      0    0
1203  AddressBookS 7.8   00:00.40   11    7   135+  6468K+ 0B     0B      1203 1
245   coreaudiod   3.8   00:19.01   4     0   264   2104K- 0B     972K+   245  1
137   WindowServer 2.9   08:43.80   4     0   377   23M-   0B-    41M+    137  1
1204  top          2.7   00:00.30   1/1   0   22+   1944K+ 0B     0B      1204 1195
1206  screencaptur 2.6   00:00.05   6     4   53+   2036K+ 20K    0B      243  243
1161  com.apple.iC 2.2   00:00.17   5     3   50+   1596K+ 0B     572K-   1161 1
92    hidd         1.9   02:01.66   7     2   94    1412K+ 0B     2508K+  92   1
265   nsurlstorage 0.7   00:01.52   4     2   95    2956K+ 0B     7468K-  265  1
1186  Terminal     0.5   00:02.50   7     1   199   13M-   0B     5772K+  1186 1
243   SystemUIServ 0.5   00:04.04   8     5   281+  4764K- 0B     3932K+  243  1
56    mds          0.4   00:21.06   8     5   255   17M-   0B     27M+    56   1
```

A. 1

B. 708

C. 243

D. 1186

118. As shown in the following image, what type of attack is being conducted?

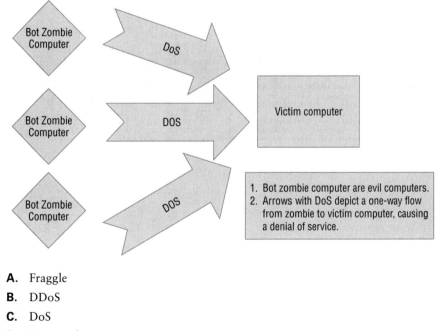

A. Fraggle

B. DDoS

C. DoS

D. Bot attack

119. What is missing to complete the three-way handshake shown here?

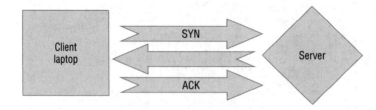

- **A.** ACK/SYN
- **B.** ACK
- **C.** TCP/IP
- **D.** SYN/ACK

120. In the following screen shot, which process is taking 386 MB of memory from the computer?

```
● ● ●                    🏠 rblockmon — top — 80×24
Processes: 178 total, 2 running, 5 stuck, 171 sleeping, 690 threads    19:56:57
Load Avg: 1.80, 1.71, 2.06  CPU usage: 2.69% user, 2.69% sys, 94.60% idle
SharedLibs: 16M resident, 17M data, 0B linkedit.
MemRegions: 38420 total, 935M resident, 39M private, 394M shared.
PhysMem: 3999M used (979M wired), 94M unused.
VM: 429G vsize, 1064M framework vsize, 0(0) swapins, 256(0) swapouts.
Networks: packets: 825122/933M in, 544300/107M out.
Disks: 88320/2643M read, 161873/4126M written.

PID   COMMAND      %CPU TIME     #TH  #WQ #PORT MEM    PURG   CMPRS  PGRP PPID
718   firefox      4.0  46:24.62 65   0   506   608M   0B     288M   718  1
0     kernel_task  2.9  10:15.34 92/4 0   2     386M   0B     0B     0    0
861   plugin-conta 5.3  08:23.21 21   0   326   110M+  0B     74M    718  718
875   soffice      0.0  03:40.23 9    1   253   93M    0B     35M    875  1
137   WindowServer 1.9  09:43.67 4    0   377   36M    44K    46M    137  1
244   Finder       0.0  00:07.46 3    0   256   21M    44K    20M    244  1
1186  Terminal     0.6  00:04.84 7    1   210   11M    0B     8004K  1186 1
215   mds_stores   0.0  00:34.61 3    1   54    11M    520K   15M    215  1
759   VTDecoderXPC 0.0  00:41.84 8    0   72    11M    0B     6660K  759  1
268   CalendarAgen 0.0  00:10.77 4    0   172   10M    0B     14M    268  1
56    mds          0.0  00:27.93 3    0   242   7964K  0B     32M    56   1
1     launchd      0.0  00:13.10 5    4   3160  7648K  0B     5700K  1    0
88    loginwindow  0.0  00:05.17 2    0   368   6640K  8192B  10M    88   1
285   Notification 0.0  00:02.23 3    0   198   6612K  0B     7340K  285  1
```

- **A.** Firefox
- **B.** kernel_task
- **C.** Finder
- **D.** WindowServer

121. What type of attack is shown in the following image?

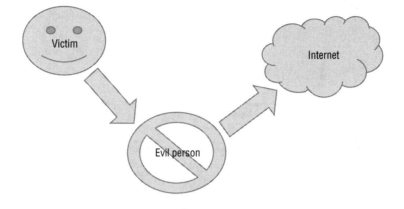

A. Man-in-the-middle

B. DoS

C. DDoS

D. Spear phishing

122. Under which scan had the most ports been scanned?

A. Ping

B. SYN stealth

C. SYN

D. DUP

123. As shown in the following screen shot, what type of algorithm was used to hash the user password?

A. SHA-512

B. Kerberos

C. AES

D. SHA-256

124. Which file or application has the permission set with 644?

A. usr

B. net

C. Volumes

D. Installer.failurerequests

125. From the information given in the Wireshark pcap file, what operating system is the source connecting to a web server?

A. OS X

B. Microsoft

C. Linux

D. Raspbian

Chapter
2

Practice Test 2

1. Which of the following is considered an administrative control?
    A. Biometric device
    B. Mantrap
    C. Security policy
    D. Access control list

2. On a class C network, how many networks can network administrators plan for if they are using the subnet mask /27?
    A. 8
    B. 32
    C. 16
    D. 1

3. What is the default port number for Telnet?
    A. 21
    B. 23
    C. 53
    D. 443

4. Convert the ASCII text *Wiley* into hexadecimal format.
    A. 57 69 6c 65 79
    B. 63 f3 1i 79 51 ab
    C. 11 fe a5 6c 81 3h
    D. 87 105 105 101 121 132

5. Which algorithm does not provide integrity or confidentiality?
    A. DSA
    B. AES
    C. RC4
    D. PGP

6. Which of the following acronyms represent the institution that governs North America IP space?
    A. ICANN
    B. PIR
    C. ARIN
    D. APNIC

7. At what layer of the OSI model does ARP reside?
    A. Presentation layer
    B. Application layer

   C. Physical layer

   D. Network layer

8. An 8-foot-tall fence with razor wire stranded on top is considered what type of measure?

   A. A deterrent measure

   B. A preventative measure

   C. A corrective measure

   D. An industrial measure

9. Which of the following standards reference the definition and implementation of wireless security such as WPA2?

   A. 802.1x

   B. 802.11ac

   C. 802.11b/g/n

   D. 802.11i

10. Which permission value in Linux allows for read and execute?

   A. 5

   B. 7

   C. 4

   D. 1

11. Which of the following correctly describes the DHCP process?

   A. Discover, offer, request, acknowledge

   B. Request, discover, offer, acknowledge

   C. Offer, acknowledge, request, discover

   D. Acknowledge, offer, request, discover

12. What key sizes in bits are used within AES?

   A. 64 and 128

   B. 128, 192, and 256

   C. 128 and 256

   D. 256

13. Which of the following describes a logic bomb?

   A. A malicious code that is delivered and executed through an email attachment

   B. Malware that is installed on the kernel operating system

   C. Malicious code that lies dormant until certain conditions are met, such as a time, date, or even certain keystrokes, and it executes its payload

   D. Malware that corrupts the CPU registers in which arbitrary code can be executed

14. Which of the following applications are mainly used to manage a botnet?

   A. IRC

   B. FTP

   C. Email

   D. Web server

15. You are team leader for your financial firm. You set a policy in place that all coworkers must clean off their desk, empty trash, shred sensitive documents, and secure other critical documents in their respective containers at the end of the day. What is the common name for such a policy?

   A. Clean room policy

   B. Clean desk policy

   C. Sanitization policy

   D. Wrapping up policy

16. You work for an organization that has its own internal network. This internal network has been extended to geographically separated company locations as well. Regardless of location, you still have access to your internal network; however, you are blocked from using the Internet because of security concerns. What type of network conditions are you experiencing?

   A. VPN

   B. Internet

   C. Extranet

   D. Intranet

17. At what layer does a circuit-level gateway operate within the OSI model?

   A. Session layer

   B. Data-Link layer

   C. Network layer

   D. Transport layer

18. Which backup method copies only those files with the bit set for archived?

   A. Full

   B. Partial

   C. Incremental

   D. Differential

19. What is another term for *masquerading*?

   A. Doppelganger

   B. Ghost

   C. Impersonation

   D. Dual persona

20. Malware installed at the kernel is very difficult to detect with products such as antivirus and anti-malware programs. What is the name of this type of malware called?

  A. Logic bomb

  B. Rootkit

  C. Vampire tap

  D. Worm

21. What is the name given for the device component physically located on the motherboard that stores encryption keys for hard drives, preventing an adversary from removing the hard drive and using it on another computer?

  A. Hard drive encryption

  B. Crypto-locker

  C. Hardware Security Module

  D. Trusted Platform Module

22. Which of the following password cracking methods is the fastest?

  A. Dictionary attack

  B. Brute force

  C. Birthday attack

  D. Reverse hash matching

23. In Linux, what designator is used to uniquely identify a user account?

  A. GID

  B. SID

  C. UID

  D. PID

24. Using Nmap, which switch command enables a UDP connections' scan of a host?

  A. -sS

  B. -sX

  C. -PT

  D. -sU

25. Which of the following best indicates a top-level parent domain?

  A. sybex.com

  B. .org

  C. www.wiley.com

  D. www.

26. Which of the following is a benefit when a security administrator is using Telnet?

  A. Traffic is sent in the clear.

  B. The password is not encrypted.

C. Security administrators can see what the adversary is doing.

D. Security administrators cannot see what the adversary is doing.

27. You are a security administrator working at a movie production company. One of your daily duties is to check the IDS logs when you are alerted. You notice that you received a lot of incomplete three-way handshakes and your memory performance has been dropping significantly on your web server and customers are complaining of really slow connections. What could be the actual issue?

    A. DoS

    B. DDoS

    C. Smurf attack

    D. SYN flood

28. What message type and code is the message "Network Unknown"?

    A. Type 3, Code 6

    B. Type 3, Code 0

    C. Type 0

    D. Type 5, Code 1

29. Which of the following frequency modes is designed to not create interference or be jammed by the adversary?

    A. Direct-sequence spread spectrum

    B. Frequency-hopping spread spectrum

    C. Orthogonal frequency-division multiplexing

    D. Time-division multiple access

30. As a security administrator, you are checking the different IP connections that are trying to contact your servers within a DMZ. You noticed months ago that your servers received very similar attacks and probes from an IP registered in Iran. This time, you notice similar tactics with IPs coming from Brazil, Greece, Sudan, and South Africa. What do you think is going on?

    A. A hacking group has banded together.

    B. Your servers on the DMZ are found to be highly attractive to hackers.

    C. A hacker is using a proxy server.

    D. You have a torrent server installed in the DMZ.

31. Which of the following provides free information about a website that includes phone numbers, administrator's email, and even the domain registration authority?

    A. Nslookup

    B. Dig

    C. Whois.net

    D. Ping

32. What is significant about RFC 18?

   A. It signifies nonroutable IP addresses.

   B. It signifies the use of web proxy servers.

   C. It describes the usage of DMZs.

   D. It covers the authentication header in IPsec.

33. Which of the following types is an ICMP echo request?

   A. Type 8

   B. Type 3, Code 1

   C. Type 0

   D. Type 5, Code 0

34. An HIDS for the most part uses which method for detection?

   A. Signature base

   B. Anomaly base

   C. Firewall rules

   D. Statistical anomaly

35. Which of the following verifies a user's authenticity when the user is requesting a certificate?

   A. Certificate authority

   B. Certificate revocation list

   C. X.509 and Kerberos

   D. Registration authority

36. A hacker is using different methods of cracking an encryption algorithm, such as side channel attacks, frequency analysis, and also bit flipping. What is the hacker doing?

   A. Brute forcing

   B. Cracking credentials

   C. Digital forensics

   D. Cryptanalysis

37. Which of the following is the correct XOR output?

   A. 0 0 = 1

   B. 1 0 = 0

   C. 1 0 = 0

   D. 1 1 = 0

38. To sniff, what mode must your network adapter be configured to in order to pull frames off an Ethernet or wireless network?

   A. Active

   B. Promiscuous

    C. Stealth

    D. CSMA/CD mode

39. Which authentication protocol is used in WPA2?

    A. CCMP

    B. 3DES

    C. AES

    D. LEAP

40. You are an administrator overseeing IT security operations for a local bank. As you review logs from the prior day, you notice a very high rate of UDP packets targeting your web server that are coming from your clients all at the same time. What could be the culprit?

    A. Smurf attack

    B. DDoS

    C. SYN flood attack

    D. Fraggle attack

41. Which is the last step in the TCP three-way handshake?

    A. ACK

    B. SYN

    C. SYN/ACK

    D. FIN

42. A token is what type of authentication factor?

    A. Type 1

    B. Type 2

    C. Type 3

    D. Type 4

43. Operating as a black hat, you decide to stand up a web server that mimics a very popular social media website. You are also a disgruntled employee who decides to build and execute a script that updates the host file on your fellow coworkers computers. It poisoned their DNS cache. Your coworkers start their morning routine by going to this popular social media website, providing their personal credentials when prompted. Unfortunately for them, they are hitting your website, and you are storing their credentials for later use. What type of attack did you conduct?

    A. Man in the middle

    B. Pharming

    C. Spear phishing

    D. Phishing

44. Which of the following is the flag byte for a TCP header used to enable an XMAS scan?

    A. 00101001

    B. 11001011

    C. 11101000

    D. 00101100

45. Which of the following describes a "soft" control?

    A. User agreement

    B. Access control list

    C. Biometrics

    D. Security clerk

46. What capability does a backdoor provide to the adversary?

    A. Backdoors can corrupt data software.

    B. They destroy cryptographic keys in the TPM.

    C. They provide low-level formatting operations.

    D. They provide remote access to the client.

47. Which of the following describes the collection of human psychical attributes for use in performing electronic authentication?

    A. Personal identification card

    B. Hair and fingerprints

    C. Biometrics

    D. Type 3 control

48. Which of the following is the only symmetric cryptography stream cipher?

    A. RC6

    B. Blowfish

    C. RC4

    D. ECE

49. Which of the following compares two hash values in order to provide nonrepudiation?

    A. DSA

    B. ECE

    C. MD5

    D. SHA-1

50. As a black hat, you identify a WAP at the mall that you are going to exploit. You discover that the WAP is using WEP. Which method will you utilize in order to exploit the WAP?

    A. The encryption algorithm, which is RC4

    B. The initialization vector (IV)

C. The password

D. The username and password

51. As a white hat who just completed the footprinting phase of your attack, you move on by operating an assortment of tools to gather intelligence on your target. You were able to determine what services are being offered on ports. You were able to see what accounts are available and to identify different sharing services as well. What phase were you operating within?

   A. Service proxy

   B. Impassive scanning

   C. Fingerprinting

   D. Enumeration

52. Using Nmap, what is the correct command to scan a target subnet of 192.168.0.0/24 using a ping sweep and identifying the operating system?

   A. `nmap -sP -O 192.168.0.0/24`

   B. `nmap -sP -V 192.168.0.0/24`

   C. `nmap -sT -P 192.168.0.0/24`

   D. `nmap -Ps -O 192.168.0.0/24`

53. Which of the following services is registered for port 110?

   A. SNMP

   B. RPC

   C. POP3

   D. LDAP

54. Which of the following is natively installed on Unix systems to conduct DNS queries?

   A. Ping

   B. Nmap

   C. Nslookup

   D. Dig

55. Which of the following sites is effective in obtaining DNS query information?

   A. `google.com`

   B. `geektools.com`

   C. `akodo-dojo.com`

   D. `yahoo.com`

56. Which of the following can you use to conduct banner grabbing?

   A. Telnet

   B. Ping

   C. `Nmap -sP`

   D. `del *.*`

57. As a pentester, what content might you include in addition to your general findings?

  A. List of patched systems

  B. List of disabled accounts

  C. List of identified vulnerabilities

  D. List of revoked certificates

58. What is the IEEE port base authentication?

  A. TACACS

  B. Diameter

  C. 802.1x

  D. TACACS+

59. Which of the following attacks sends fragmented UDP packets to a Windows system using port 53 or other UDP ports that may cause the system to crash?

  A. Fraggle

  B. Bonk

  C. Smash the stack

  D. Smurf

60. Which of the following is an application that does not need a host or human interaction to disrupt and corrupt data?

  A. Worm

  B. Virus

  C. Trojan

  D. Malware

61. A user reports that they are receiving pop-up window advertisements that occur randomly. There are even times when there are so many windows that the user is forced to restart the computer. What could be the issue?

  A. A Trojan is installed on her workstation.

  B. Adware is installed.

  C. The website that is generating the pop ups is still running.

  D. There is a rootkit installed.

62. Which of the following describes the level at which a business or an organization can defend against and withstand a cyberattack?

  A. Defense in depth

  B. Security measure

  C. Baseline configuration

  D. Security posture

63. What is one disadvantage of a single sign-on (SSO) strategy?

    A. It offers a single point of failure for authentication.

    B. There is no replication for security policies.

    C. Passwords are stored in plain text.

    D. User accounts are easily accessible.

64. What authentication factor is based on where you are located?

    A. Type 1

    B. Type 2

    C. Type 3

    D. Type 4

65. Which of the following is an optimal way of discovering passwords in plain text?

    A. Intercepting an SSH connection

    B. Following a TCP stream

    C. Intercepting SSL traffic

    D. Cracking an account using John the Ripper

66. What is a content-addressable memory table?

    A. A table of IP addresses

    B. A table used to view NetBIOS names

    C. A table of MAC addresses pertaining to ports

    D. A list of domain names tied to IP addresses

67. A black hat sends fragments of an ICMP message to a victim's system. When the system receives all of the packets, it reassembles them and then it crashes. Which attack would cause such behavior?

    A. Ping of death

    B. DoS

    C. Fraggle attack

    D. ICMP flood

68. Which of the following uses symmetric keys in its SSO authentication standard.

    A. SESAME

    B. Diameter

    C. Kerberos

    D. HIDS

69. What is the protocol that changes a private IP address to a public address at the gateway?

    A. NAT

    B. PAT

    C. GNAT

    D. NAT-T

70. Which combination is used in intrusion detection systems?

    A. NIDS and SIDS

    B. HIDS and SIDS

    C. IDS and IPS

    D. HIDS and NIDS

71. You are a security administrator tasked with determining the expected losses a media firm may incur in the event of a fire. You estimate the firm could expect to lose half of its assets, equal to $10 million dollars. You also determine that the likelihood of a fire occurring is once every 10 years. What is the annual loss expectancy (ALE)?

    A. Loss of $500,000

    B. Loss of $1,000,000

    C. Gain of $250,000

    D. Loss of $250,000

72. Which federal law mandates securing medical records at rest and in transit?

    A. PCI

    B. HIPAA

    C. FISMA

    D. PATRIOT Act

73. What is one advantage an attacker (black hat) has over a defender (potential victim)?

    A. Time

    B. Online hacking forums

    C. Money

    D. Metasploit

74. Which of the following is associated with security access in a wireless network?

    A. WPA

    B. 802.1x

    C. Radius

    D. TACACS+

75. Which of the following deletes the Clients table within a SQL database?

    A. `UPDATE TABLE Clients`

    B. `SELECT * FROM Clients`

    C. `INSERT TABLE Clients`

    D. `DROP TABLE Clients`

76. Which of the following tools is used to scan for vulnerabilities on a target system or a network?

    A. Snort

    B. Ncat

    C. Nessus

    D. Metasploit

77. As a security administrator, you have security concerns regarding the plans to utilize wireless networks to bridge different corporate offices. Due to the location of these offices, traditional connections are cost prohibitive. Which of the following antennas will provide the best coverage while limiting the probability of unwanted signal interception?

    A. Omni

    B. Fan

    C. Yagi

    D. Satellite dish

78. Which of the following encryption methods was developed by Phil Zimmerman?

    A. AES

    B. PGP

    C. DES

    D. DEA

79. What addressing scheme is used by IPv6?

    A. 32 bits

    B. 128 bytes

    C. 32 bytes

    D. 128 bits

80. Which of the following best describes a vulnerability?

    A. A threat being potentially realized

    B. No countermeasure available

    C. A threat actor

    D. An incident

81. A new user in a company is given a minimal set of privileges. As they are promoted and move to different positions, they continue to gain more privileges. What is this called?

    A. Scope creep

    B. Position creep

    C. Access creep

    D. Privilege escalation

82. What would you call a device on a network?

   A. A node

   B. A computer

   C. A switch

   D. An access device

83. What would you call an application that secretly collects information about a victim?

   A. Trojan

   B. Spyware

   C. Malware

   D. Stealware

84. How many characters does a service set identifier (SSID) contain?

   A. 32

   B. 64

   C. 20

   D. 128

85. What is the purpose of the Internet Key Exchange (IKE) protocol?

   A. To transfer user data

   B. To collect user profiles

   C. To distribute keys to the public

   D. To exchange secret keys

86. In regard to biometrics, when the false reject rate (FRR) and the false acceptance rate (FAR) are equal, what does this intersection mean?

   A. Crossover error rate

   B. False equal rate

   C. Sum

   D. Crossover equal rate

87. An application that is designed to look like a known legitimate application, but is actuality malicious in nature is considered what type of malware?

   A. Spyware

   B. Rootkit

   C. Adware

   D. Trojan

88. What standard port does SFTP use?

   A. 20

   B. 21

    C. 22

    D. 20 and 21

89. Which of the following describes an IEEE 802.3 environment?

    A. CSMA/CD

    B. Wireless security

    C. User access control list

    D. Port base authentication

90. You are a system administrator for a law firm. You are informed that a few users are indicating that anytime they enter their email address when opening applications, their computer requires a manual reboot in order to recover a system fault according to a pop-up window. What could be the problem?

    A. A Trojan was executed.

    B. A logic bomb was initiated.

    C. The users do not have patience.

    D. The users were in a middle of patch update.

91. Which of the following services is associated with TCP port 389?

    A. LDAP

    B. IMAP

    C. SMB

    D. RPC

92. A system creates a certificate with the assigned public and private keys. This system also digitally signs it. What is this system's role?

    A. Registering authority

    B. Certificate authority

    C. Kerberos system

    D. Server/client environment

93. As a security administrator, you want to restrict employee access to information to only certain individuals. What type of access will you implement?

    A. Need to know

    B. Least privilege

    C. Reducing availability

    D. Setting up an encryption process

94. Microsoft Office and other office suite applications have a feature that should be turned off to prevent malware from executing or spreading. What feature should be disabled?

    A. Mail

    B. FTP client

    C. Auto-update feature

    D. Macro feature

95. What is the name of the entity that is certified to hold trusted keys?

    A. Government safe

    B. Hot site

    C. Escrow

    D. Offsite backup

96. What standard TCP port does HTTPS use?

    A. 443

    B. 8080

    C. 80

    D. 22

97. When a user authenticates once to a resource and is then permitted to access additional applications without the need to reauthenticate, what form of authentication is being used?

    A. Once sign-on

    B. Nonce sign-on

    C. Kerberos

    D. Single sign-on

98. What does a router separate?

    A. Collision domains

    B. Broadcast domains

    C. Switching domains

    D. Routing loops

99. What UDP port is Type 0 associated with?

    A. It is associated with port 53.

    B. It uses the entire port range, that is, 0 to 1023.

    C. ICMP is not associated with port numbers.

    D. Ports are generated dynamically for Type 0.

100. Which of the following storage technologies is considered the most volatile?

    A. Hard drive

    B. USB flash drive

    C. CPU cache

    D. DDR3

101. The password file of a Windows system is located in which of the following directories?

A. `C:\System32\Windows\config`

B. `\etc\win\config`

C. `C:\System\Windows\config`

D. `C:\Windows\System32\config`

102. What is the act of guessing every possible password combination of an account?

A. Brute force

B. Pass the hash

C. Dictionary attack

D. Social engineering

103. What command would you use to give read, write, and execute privileges for an object to the owner, group, and others in Linux?

A. `chmod 666`

B. `chmod 777`

C. `chmod 7`

D. `chmod 532`

104. In Linux, which of the following is used to toggle between the different operating systems to boot from?

A. Unified Bootloader

B. Ctrl+S

C. Grand Unified Bootloader

D. Ctrl+F4+S

105. Which of the following is considered a framework for penetration testing of a system?

A. Metasploit

B. Cain & Abel

C. Nessus

D. Security Onion

106. In Windows, what command can you use to hide a file?

A. `+h attrib <filename>`

B. `h+ <filename>`

C. `filename attrib +h`

D. `attrib +h <filename>`

107. Which of the following is a correct MAC address?

    A. 00-12-3e-ff-d4-98

    B. 3i-45-fa-90-25-1b

    C. ff-ff-ff-ff-ff-ff-fg

    D. 65-23-ab-cb-a9

108. A packet firewall device operates at what layer of the OSI model?

    A. Layer 2

    B. Layer 4

    C. Layer 7

    D. Layer 3

109. As a black hat, you are scanning an array of subnets and determine that you have found one that is lacking some security appliances. You also determine that there are obvious signs of misconfiguration or a lack of detail. It may be possible the administrator is a rookie and still learning the ropes on hardening their network. What could possibly be the issue here?

    A. Honeynet

    B. Honeypot

    C. Misconfiguration

    D. A subnet that's not in use anymore

110. What is the biggest drawback from using anti-malware software?

    A. It takes up processing resources.

    B. It must have up-to-date virus definitions.

    C. Anti-malware software is expensive.

    D. It can be centrally or independently administered.

111. What is the name of the DES algorithm?

    A. DEA

    B. DES

    C. Twofish

    D. 3DES

112. What does Heartbleed provide to the adversary?

    A. The memory contents of the target server at the time of exploit

    B. A DoS

    C. The adversary's memory contents at the time

    D. It does not provide any information to the adversary.

113. A user reports that they have downloaded a music file from the Internet. They inform you that when they opened the file, it seemed as though it installed an application, and then the user was prompted to send a payment of $500 dollars to a PayPal account to get the key to unencrypt their hard drive. The user no longer has access to their desktop. What could be the issue?

    A. The user is experiencing a hoax.

    B. The user downloaded and installed ransomware.

    C. The user installed malware.

    D. The user downloaded the wrong music file.

114. Which Wi-Fi standard has a radio band of 2.4 and 5 GHz and a speed of 100 Mbps?

    A. 802.11i

    B. 802.11

    C. 802.b

    D. 802.11n

115. What type of infrastructure does this describe?

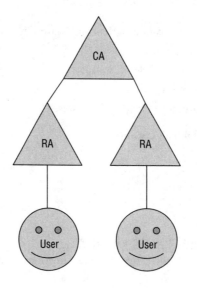

    A. PKI

    B. Man-in-the-middle attack

    C. Social engineering

    D. Kerberos environment

116. What type of protocol is primarily being used in this diagram?

A. Broadcast

B. ARP request

C. Ping

D. DHCP lease

117. What IP address can you determine from the following diagram?

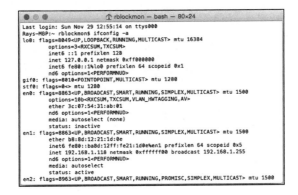

A. 192.168.1.255

B. 192.168.1.118

C. 255.255.255.255

D. 192.168.1.1

118. What encoding type is being used in the screen shot?

- **A.** ASCII
- **B.** Hexadecimal
- **C.** Binary format
- **D.** UTF-8

119. What TLS version can be found in the following screen shot?

    A.   1.2

    B.   1.3

    C.   312

    D.   1

120. What is the adversary trying to do in the following diagram?

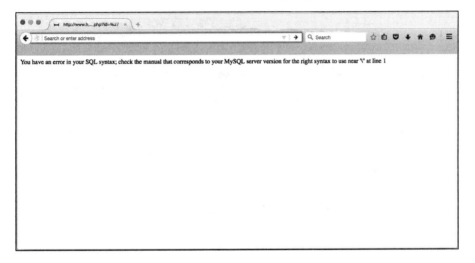

    A.   Ping of death

    B.   Web server detection

    C.   SQL injection

    D.   Web defacement

121. As seen in the following screen shot, what is the adversary trying to do in URL bar in the web browser?

You have an error in your SQL syntax; check the manual that corresponds to your MySQL server version for the right syntax to use near '\' at line 1

- **A.** Privilege escalation
- **B.** Directory traversal
- **C.** Blind SQL injection
- **D.** Deletion of a table in SQL

122. What DNS system is being queried by the client in the following screen shot?

- **A.** Google
- **B.** Port 53
- **C.** Port 64234
- **D.** None

123. What is the password for the user root according to the following screen shot?

- **A.** Root
- **B.** x
- **C.** There is no password.
- **D.** x:0:0

124. Based on the following log in Snort, what is the destination port to which the file is being downloaded?

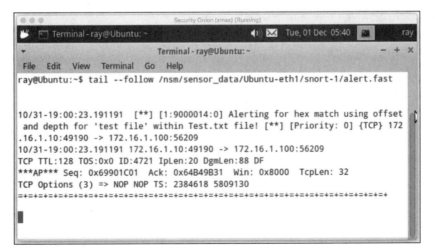

A. 56209

B. 23

C. 49190

D. The port is not available.

125. Which of the following is a user account?

```
colord:x:16733:0:99999:7:::
lightdm:x:16733:0:99999:7:::
avahi-autoipd:x:16733:0:99999:7:::
avahi:x:16733:0:99999:7:::
usbmux:x:16733:0:99999:7:::
kernoops:x:16733:0:99999:7:::
pulse:x:16733:0:99999:7:::
rtkit:x:16733:0:99999:7:::
speech-dispatcher:x:16733:0:99999:7:::
hplip:x:16733:0:99999:7:::
saned:x:16733:0:99999:7:::
mysql:x:16733:0:99999:7:::
ntp:x:16733:0:99999:7:::
sshd:x:16733:0:99999:7:::
sphinxsearch:x:16733:0:99999:7:::
prads:x:16733:0:99999:7:::
ossec:x:16733:0:99999:7:::
ossecm:x:16733:0:99999:7:::
ossecr:x:16733:0:99999:7:::
nobody:x:16733:0:99999:7:::
ray:$6$xHEKhMr2$95xeLgwRrKfDZ7QvhhGSt3bn2xFSqETvLgWJVJd7VcQiOj./eXJh4CG9fF1ls
yJu3E2Mvlno/iYxPocUNHrYd/:16733:0:99999:7:::
sguil:!:16739:0:99999:7:::
```

A. usbmux

B. ray

C. ossecr

D. nobody

Chapter
3

Practice Test 3

1. Which protocol is used for network management and can gather statistics and derive a current status from the node that it is operating on?

    A. NTP

    B. SMNP

    C. SSH

    D. SNMP

2. Which of the following is part of a DMZ but bridges access from organization to organization?

    A. Internet

    B. Extranet

    C. Intranet

    D. Outernet

3. How many subnets can be provided using a /26 classless inter-domain routing (CIDR)?

    A. 1

    B. 2

    C. 3

    D. 4

4. In a Linux system, where is the password file stored?

    A. /etc/passwd

    B. /etc/shadow

    C. /etc/user/password

    D. /shadow/etc

5. What command can you use to switch to a different user in Linux?

    A. swu

    B. user

    C. sudo

    D. su

6. What encryption algorithm is used within TLS?

    A. AES

    B. RSA

    C. PGP

    D. ECE

7. Prior to deploying an anomaly-based detection system on a network, what must be achieved?

    A. Baseline

    B. Updated file definition

C. Updated network infrastructure

D. Patches pushed to clients before installation

8. Which of the following records determines a mail server in your domain?

A. SOA

B. CNAME

C. A

D. MX

9. Which of the following has the least amount of memory available?

A. DIMM

B. SIMM

C. CPU cache

D. DDR3

10. You are a security administrator for a local bank. You notice that some of the employees have been in their current positions for quite some time. What risk could possibly occur based on this situation?

A. Employees that held positions for a long time can circumvent security measures.

B. Workers can skip out on work easily.

C. Employees know too much about their job.

D. Workers can develop and understand other workers' work habits.

11. You are a security administrator for an online dating website. Your website recently experienced a zero day SSL attack that leaked information about your SQL database. As an immediate course of action, what would be your first choice in defending and keeping your client's information safe?

A. Update all the web servers with the latest virus definitions.

B. Put up a maintenance banner on the front page and restrict all Internet traffic.

C. Change PKI certificates.

D. Install the latest patches to clients immediately on the workstations.

12. The SAM log file entry is located in what part of a Windows Registry system?

A. HKEY_LOCAL_MACHINE\SAM

B. HKEY_LOCAL_SAM

C. HKEY_LOCAL_MACHINE\WINDOWS

D. HKEY_SYSTEM_MACHINE\SAME.L

13. Under which auxiliary in Metasploit can you scan for SNMP configurations?

A. `auxiliary/snmp/scanner`

B. `auxiliary/snmp/version`

C. `auxiliary/scanner/snmp`

D. `auxiliary/scan/snmp`

14. In Linux, what command is used to search for information?

    A. ser

    B. grep

    C. info >

    D. ls -l

15. Which of the following tools is used to encode your payload in Metasploit?

    A. msfconsole

    B. msfpayload

    C. encodesploit

    D. msfencode

16. A system is compromised and is able to spawn a connection back to the adversary. What is the common term used to describe this activity?

    A. Reverse shellcode

    B. reverse socket

    C. Victim-initiated shellcode

    D. Call to attacker shellcode

17. What do buffers contain?

    A. Infinite data

    B. Data storage capacity

    C. Data in transit

    D. Processing power

18. What type of function is being called by strcpy (attacker, "exploit_this");?

    A. strcpy

    B. ( );

    C. The variable, which is attacker

    D. None

19. What is the issue when there is no boundary being checked or validated in programming?

    A. The program will assign its own values.

    B. The program does not validate if the input values can be stored without overwriting the next memory segment.

    C. The program executes without checking what other programs are open.

    D. Memory allocation has already been reserved for a program.

20. When writing a program, what is one of the fundamental tasks that should be done when declaring a variable?

    A. Assign a random value to it.

    B. Do not assign a value because it can corrupt data.

   C. Initialize the variable.

   D. A variable does not need to be initialized.

21. What is a heap?

   A. A static allocation of memory

   B. A memory segment located within the CPU

   C. Memory that is swapped with using the hard drive

   D. Memory allocation of size and location that is assigned dynamically

22. What is the region in memory that is assigned to a process or a program when it is initiated?

   A. Cluster

   B. Stack

   C. Heap

   D. Pointer

23. What can the adversary do in order to get around a segment violation when trying to execute their own code in memory?

   A. Use padding to increase the chances of finding the correct address using NOP.

   B. Statically assign a return address to the pointer.

   C. Smash the stack.

   D. Dynamically assign values in memory to receive a point address.

24. Which term defines the condition when an adversary purposely crashes a server?

   A. Smashing the stack

   B. Server crashing

   C. Denial of service

   D. Buffer overflow

25. Which of the following protocols is/are vulnerable to session hijacking?

   A. TCP/IP

   B. UDP/IP

   C. Man-in-the-middle attack

   D. IP

26. Which of the following must be conducted first in order to hijack a session?

   A. Track the session.

   B. Desynchronize the session.

   C. Inject the adversary's packet into the stream.

   D. Disrupt the stream first and then inject the adversary's packet information.

27. Which standard provides best business practice for information security management?

    A. ISO 27002

    B. ISO 21999

    C. OWASP

    D. BBB

28. Which of the following is used for recording key strokes at a terminal or keyboard using malicious software?

    A. Spyware

    B. Malware

    C. Key logger

    D. Recordware

29. Within SNMP, which of the following is used for authentication?

    A. PIN

    B. Asymmetric strings

    C. Community strings

    D. Cryptographic strings

30. What is the function of a CNAME record?

    A. Provides authentication to a website

    B. Encrypts DNS zone transfers

    C. Supplements an alias to a domain name

    D. Replaces the MX for security transactions

31. Software that creates pop-up advertisement messages while visiting websites is known as what?

    A. Adware

    B. Malware

    C. Pop-up blocker

    D. Freeware

32. The ability for information or services that must be accessible at a moment's notices is called what?

    A. Survivability

    B. Availability

    C. CIA

    D. Redundancy

33. A device that facilitates connections and acts as a middleman between a trusted zone and an untrusted zone is referred to as what?

    A. Firewall

    B. Man in the middle

C. Gateway

D. Proxy server

34. Which of the following provides steganography?

A. XPtools

B. EtherApe

C. Wireshark

D. Cain

35. Which of the following tools can be used to DDoS a target system?

A. LOIC

B. SIMM

C. Cain & Abel

D. AOL Punter

36. In SQL, which of the following allows an individual to update a table?

A. DROP

B. ADD

C. COPY

D. UPDATE

37. In Linux, besides the User and Group, what other object can be assigned permissions?

A. Domain

B. Realm

C. Others

D. All others

38. Of the following, which allows you to conduct password cracking?

A. LOIC

B. John the Ripper

C. CPU Dump

D. Wireshark

39. In the TCP/IP model, what is the equivalent of the OSI Network layer?

A. Network

B. Internet

C. Transport

D. Network Access

40. What flag is used to order a connection to terminate?

A. SYN

B. FIN

C. PSH

D. RST

41. Which of the following scanners provides ping sweeps and at times can be very noisy if not properly configured?

A. Angry IP

B. Cain & Abel

C. `nmap -sT -T0`

D. Nslookup

42. Which of the following is an application that provides ARP spoofing?

A. Cain & Abel

B. Evercrack

C. Kismet

D. John the Ripper

43. A team that conducts penetration testing can be referred to as what?

A. Blue team

B. Red team

C. Black team

D. White team

44. Which option describes an adversary pretending to be someone else in order to obtain credit or attempt fraud?

A. Impersonation

B. Identity Theft

C. Masquerading

D. Cloning

45. Which Linux distribution is best suited to support an attacker by providing the necessary preinstalled tools?

A. Kali

B. Security Onion

C. Mint

D. Ubuntu

46. Which of the following is conducted during the pre-attack phase of a pen test?

A. Clearing logs

B. Elevating privileges

C. Reconnaissance

D. Acquiring a target

47. Which of the following organizations provides government-backed standards?

   A. EC-Council

   B. NIST

   C. CAIN

   D. NITS

48. Which of the following teams is a group of people focused on addressing or resolving key issues or problems in an organization, often in a temporary state of structure?

   A. Tiger team

   B. Red team

   C. Project management team

   D. Project sponsor

49. When a user or a process is trying to evade security mechanisms and policies, it uses what type of channel?

   A. Overt

   B. Dark

   C. Espionage or secret

   D. Covert

50. What is a Type 0 ICMP message?

   A. ECHO request

   B. ICMP request

   C. Ping reply

   D. ECHO reply

51. Which wireless mode is used when there is a point-to-point connection but no wireless access point involved?

   A. One to one

   B. Synchronization setting

   C. Ad hoc

   D. Clients must access a WAP

52. To sniff wireless traffic, what must you have set on your wireless adapter?

   A. Transport mode

   B. AirPcap mode

   C. Transparency mode

   D. Promiscuous mode

53. In social engineering, what is one of the things that the adversary will try to accomplish?

   A. Manipulation

   B. Conducting a man-in-the-middle attack

    C. Copy the user's email account.

    D. Forwarding the user's web access to the adversary's website

54. When a system or a process lacks a countermeasure, what is it considered?

    A. Secured

    B. A threat

    C. A threat agent or threat vector

    D. Vulnerable

55. An ATM transaction uses which type of authentication method(s)?

    A. Type 2

    B. Something you have

    C. Type 1 and Type 2

    D. Token with a PIN assigned

56. In what situation would you immediately exercise a password change policy?

    A. Every 90 days

    B. When an account may be compromised

    C. When a user has been on vacation for two weeks

    D. When a user account has been disabled

57. Firewalls work on which type of default policy?

    A. Implicit allow all.

    B. Block all ICMP.

    C. Block all incoming traffic.

    D. Implicit deny all.

58. Which tool is used to illuminate a SID for a username?

    A. Nslookup

    B. SID2User

    C. HKEY_LOCAL_USER\SID

    D. >user ls -l

59. On which port does a standard DNS zone transfer operate?

    A. 53

    B. 80

    C. 8080

    D. 25

60. The process of dialing unsecured modems at random is called what?

    A. War dialing

    B. Blue boxing

    C. Black boxing

    D. Modem pinging

61. What UDP flag forces a connection to terminate at both ends of the circuit?

    A. RST

    B. FIN

    C. None

    D. URG and RST

62. What information does the traceroute tool provide?

    A. Username of the person logged in

    B. What links are encrypted on the network

    C. Layer 3 protocol details

    D. Route path information and hop count

63. What does the TLL value mean?

    A. The number of packets remaining until it times out

    B. The number of hops to the destination

    C. The number of the packet last sent

    D. The number of routing loops that are permitted

64. Which of the following delegates a DNS zone?

    A. EX

    B. NS

    C. EM

    D. PTR

65. Which of the following switches enables an idle scan within the Nmap tool?

    A. `-Si`

    B. `-sI`

    C. `-Is`

    D. None, because Nmap does not support idle scans

66. What process methodology is used to measure the potential performance with actual performance?

    A. Baseline analysis

    B. Statistical analysis

    C. Gap analysis

    D. Trend analysis

67. A data center (site) that is fully operational and can begin processing in the event of a catastrophic event is what type of site?

A. Warm site

B. Backup site

C. Mirror site

D. Hot site

68. What does a router separate?

A. Collision domains

B. Subnets

C. Networks

D. Broadcast domains

69. A key that is known to only one person is called what?

A. Asymmetric encryption

B. Symmetric encryption

C. Private key

D. Secret key

70. When an administrator wants to bind two pieces of hardware together, what hardware would they use to bind them using cryptographic measures?

A. TPM

B. Block cipher

C. Encryption keys

D. Encryption module

71. What tool can be used to spoof a MAC address?

A. MAC and Cheese

B. Cheesy MAC

C. GodSMAC

D. SMAC

72. What type of antenna focuses the direction of the signal?

A. Yagi

B. Omni

C. Small aperture

D. LOIC

73. Which of the following encrypts community strings and provides authentication?

A. ICMP

B. SNMPv3 (Simple Network Management Protocol)

C. SNMP

D. IMAP

74. A wireless access point that looks legitimate may actually be what?

A. Rogue AP

B. Man in the middle

C. Ad hoc solution

D. Evil twin

75. Which of the following malware achieved a historical first by causing physical damage to a nuclear reactor facility?

A. Stuxnet

B. Blue's Revenge

C. ILOVEYOU virus

D. Back Orifice

76. What does a wrapper provide an attacker with?

A. A way to conceal malware within a package that the victim won't mind opening

B. A way to conceal cryptographic keys

C. A way to disrupt user's data

D. A way to corrupt user's data

77. Lights, bollards, and fences are part of what type of control?

A. Technical - External

B. Soft

C. Management

D. Physical - External

78. What type of attack does POODLE invoke?

A. Denial of service

B. Man in the middle

C. Distributed denial of service

D. Credential harvesting

79. What is another name for Tor?

A. The other router

B. The onion router

C. TLS open router

D. Tunnel open router

80. In Kerberos, which of the following grants access to a service?

A. Ticket-granting ticket

B. Ticket authentication service

C. Ticket-granting service

D. Ticket granted access

81. What must a signature-based IDS have in order to be effective?

A. An up-to-date signature list

B. A baseline

C. Active rules

D. Access to update user profiles

82. What type of timer does an Ethernet network use to prevent collisions?

A. Broadcast domains

B. Collision domains

C. Backoff timer

D. Hold-off timer

83. Who were the first ones to discover the POODLE vulnerability?

A. Phil Zimmerman

B. Akodo Toturi

C. Urza and Mishra

D. Moller, Duong, and Kotowicz

84. What is the Common Vulnerabilities and Exposures (CVE) identification issued for Heartbleed?

A. CVE-2014-0809

B. CVE-2014-0160

C. CVE-2015-0160

D. There are no CVEs associated with Heartbleed.

85. Which report would be best given to a client's senior leadership team?

A. Analysis report

B. Project summary report

C. Executive summary report

D. Chapter summary report

86. What is the security principle that requires two people in order to perform a task?

A. Least privilege

B. Two-man source

C. Biba Model

D. Separation of duties

87. As a security administrator, you are conducting corrective actions against a system that crashed due to malicious code. What is this activity called?

    A. System hardening

    B. Remediation

    C. Patching

    D. Fix action

88. A Category I IAVA (information assurance vulnerability alert) is equal to what?

    A. Inevitable compromise

    B. System infected with data destruction malware

    C. Root system access

    D. Ransomware that was installed

89. As a network administrator, your manager instructs you to reduce the organization's accessibility to the file server. She claims that doing so will aid in preventing company trade secrets from being leaked to the public; however, you understand that doing so will have a negative impact on productivity and aggravate employees. Which part of the Confidentiality, Integrity, and Availability triad is being impacted here?

    A. Integrity

    B. Confidentially

    C. Least privilege/need to know

    D. Availability

90. As a CISO, you published a security policy to your organization that a cross-shred shredder must be used to destroy classified documents in a secure manner. What type of security control did you implement?

    A. Technical

    B. Physical

    C. Administrative

    D. Controlled destruction

91. Which of the following is the most common Network Access Translation protocol used??

    A. S-NAT

    B. PAT

    C. Basic NAT

    D. Public NAT

92. Due to the ILOVEYOUvirus, Microsoft implemented a new business practice in its software to prevent such attacks from occurring again. What was it?

    A. Disabling the macro features in Microsoft Office by default

    B. Disabling the CD-ROM autorun feature

    C. Setting user profiles to disabled

    D. Removing HEKY_LOCAL_MACHINE\USER

93. What kind of control would you use to validate and authenticate a user based on their physical location?

   A. Type 1

   B. Something you are

   C. Type 4

   D. GPS tracking

94. Which of the following denotes the root directory in a Linux system?

   A. root/

   B. /

   C. home\

   D. \home\

95. As the security administrator, you are tasked with implementing an access control strategy that will assign permissions to users based on the roles they will be hired to fill. What type of access control are you being asked to implement for your organization?

   A. RBAC

   B. MAC

   C. DAC

   D. UAC

96. As a black hat, you are conducting a reconnaissance operation on a potential target. You gather intelligence by using publicly available information, conducting stakeouts of the facility, and observing workers as they enter and leave the premises from across the street. What phase of the hacking methodologies are you operating within?

   A. Footprinting

   B. Fingerprinting

   C. Active surveillance

   D. Passive reconnaissance

97. In Snort, which part of the rule dictates the source, destination, rule type, and direction?

   A. Rule body

   B. Rule action

   C. Rule head

   D. Rule connection

98. What prevents IP packets from circulating throughout the Internet forever?

   A. TTL

   B. Spanning tree

   C. Broadcast domains

   D. NAT

99. As a white hat, you are conducting an audit of your customer's security policies. You notice that the policies the organization published do not conform to its actual practices. You also note that the security administrators are implementing different corrective actions than what is supposed to be happening according to the policies. What is the correct action to take here?

   A. Inform the security administrators that they need to follow the security policies published by the organization.

   B. Recommend a once-a-month meeting that evaluates and make changes to the security policies.

   C. Allow the security administrators to tailor their practices as they see fit.

   D. Shred the old policies.

100. As a black hat, you are trying to prevent an IDS from alerting your presence to the network administrators. You determine that the rules that are set in place by the firewall are pretty effective and you dare not risk any more attempts to get past the security appliances. What is one method that may defeat the security policies set in place by the IDS and other security appliances?

   A. Firewalking

   B. Conducting a reverse shell exploit

   C. Session splicing

   D. Encrypting your traffic

101. When a layer 2 switch is flooded, what mode does it default to?

   A. Fail open mode, where it mimics a hub.

   B. Fail closed, where nothing is passed anymore.

   C. Layer 2 switches process IP packets and not datagrams.

   D. Layer 2 switches cannot be flooded because they are collision domains.

102. Using Nmap, what switches allow us to fingerprint an operating system and conduct a port scan?

   A. -sS -sO

   B. -sSO

   C. -O -Ss

   D. -O -sS

103. Which application allows the adversary to conduct war dialing for vulnerable systems using a modem?

   A. Blue Box

   B. ToneLoc

   C. TwoTone

   D. Icy Manipulator

104. Using ACK in TCP, if there was no response, what can we determine from the port?

   A. ACK does not use a port.

   B. The port is open and ready to receive a SYN packet.

   C. The port is closed.

   D. A SYN/ACK is returned.

105. As a security administrator, you are responsible for leading a working group on determining threats that pose a significant risk to your assets that are intangible. What type of analysis are you conducting?

   A. Quantitative risk analysis

   B. Risk mitigation analysis

   C. Qualitative risk analysis

   D. Qualitative risk mitigation

106. Which of the following describes a wireless band that operates at 11 Mbps and uses the 2.4 GHz frequency?

   A. 802.11b

   B. 802.11

   C. 802.11g

   D. 802.11a

107. IPv6 uses IPsec. Which of the following establishes the key agreement?

   A. IKE

   B. ISAKMP

   C. Diffie-Hellman

   D. TLS

108. What ICMP type denotes a "Time Exceeded" response?

   A. Type 3

   B. Type 0

   C. Type 5

   D. Type 11

109. Which of the following is a lightweight Cisco proprietary protocol for building security tunnels?

   A. EAP

   B. PEAP

   C. CHAP

   D. LEAP

110. What three services are usually included with the NETBIOS protocol?

    A. NBT, NetBIOS session, and NetBIOS datagram

    B. NBT, asymmetric session, and NetBIOS datagram

    C. NetBIOS datagram, NBT, and NetBIOS AD

    D. NetBIOS datagram, NBT, and NetBIOS SCP

111. Which vulnerability exploits Cisco's LEAP?

    A. LEAPER

    B. ASLEAP

    C. CLEAP

    D. REAP

112. What do wireless access points use to advertise their presence?

    A. Beacon frame

    B. Homing beacon

    C. Homing broadcast

    D. Broadcast frame

113. As a security administrator, you notice that your users are writing down their login credentials and sticking them on their monitors. What is an effective way of combating this security issue?

    A. Implementing a PKI solution

    B. Mandate password changes every 30 days.

    C. Set up a user and security awareness training session.

    D. Inform users that they need to memorize their credentials.

114. What does stateful inspection provide to the network administrator?

    A. It tracks all communication streams and the packets are inspected.

    B. It provides the administrator with a slower network response.

    C. It ensures that communications are terminated.

    D. It provides the administrator with reduced admin work.

115. As a white hat, you're tasked to identify all vulnerabilities possible on a network segment that your customer provided to you. Although you are given nothing but a subnet mask to reference, nothing else has been provided. What type of assessment are you conducting?

    A. White box

    B. Gray box

    C. Black box

    D. Crystal box

116. What is wrong with the following diagram?

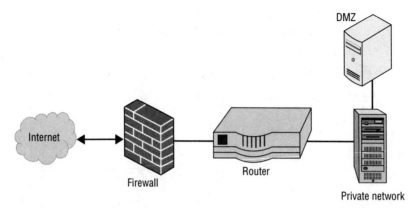

- **A.** There is no subnet being screened.
- **B.** The firewall should be behind the router.
- **C.** The DMZ should be in front of the private network.
- **D.** The DMZ should be associated with the Internet. The DMZ should reside off of the firewall and not directly off of the private network.

117. What type of network topology is being shown in the following diagram?

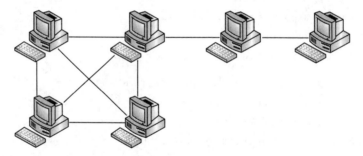

- **A.** Token ring topology
- **B.** Hybrid-mesh topology
- **C.** Bus topology
- **D.** Screen subnet

118. What type of subnet is being implemented based on this logical diagram?

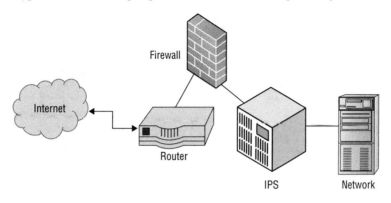

- **A.** Dual-homed firewall
- **B.** Double-screen firewall
- **C.** Screen subnet
- **D.** Screen firewall

119. What is missing from the TCP segment structure?

SOURCE PORT		DESTINATION PORT	
SEQUENCE NUMBER			
ACKNOWLEDGE NUMBER			
OFFSET	RESERVED	??????????	WINDOW
CHECKSUM			
OPTIONS		PADDING	
DATA			

- **A.** Timing
- **B.** TTL
- **C.** ICMP
- **D.** Flags

120. What would be the last values to complete the connection?

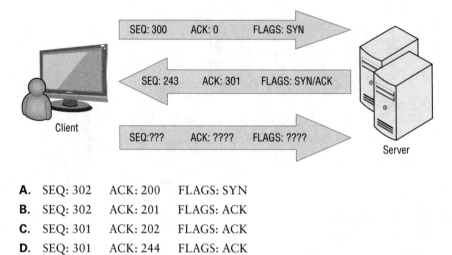

A. SEQ: 302   ACK: 200   FLAGS: SYN
B. SEQ: 302   ACK: 201   FLAGS: ACK
C. SEQ: 301   ACK: 202   FLAGS: ACK
D. SEQ: 301   ACK: 244   FLAGS: ACK

121. What type of application has impacted Ring 0?

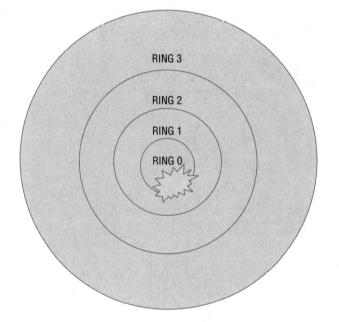

A. Root access
B. Malware
C. Rootkit
D. Trojan virus

122. The following depicts the adversary conducting what type of action?

   A. Passive reconnaissance
   B. Scanning and enumeration
   C. Footprinting
   D. Fingerprinting

123. What type of attack is the adversary conducting in the following diagram?

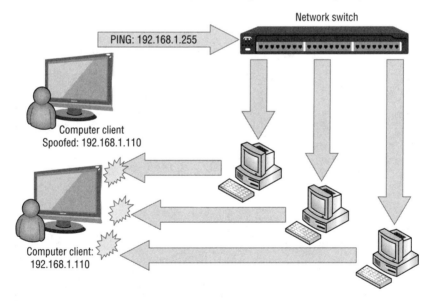

   A. Smurf attack
   B. Bluesnarfing
   C. Teardrop attack
   D. DoS attack

124. What type of attack is the adversary conducting in the following diagram?

Bad guy   Good guy

- **A.** Man-in-the-middle attack
- **B.** Shoulder surfing
- **C.** Passive reconnaissance
- **D.** Foot inactive surveillance

125. In the following screen shot, why is the packet flag set to "Don't Fragment"?

```
                              Wi-Fi: en1
 Apply a display filter ... <#/>                                      Expression...  +
▶ Frame 112: 395 bytes on wire (3160 bits), 395 bytes captured (3160 bits) on interface 0
▼ Ethernet II, Src: SamsungE_23:e6:b5 (c0:bd:d1:23:e6:b5), Dst: Apple_21:1d:0e (b8:8d:12:21:1d:0e)
  ▶ Destination: Apple_21:1d:0e (b8:8d:12:21:1d:0e)
  ▶ Source: SamsungE_23:e6:b5 (c0:bd:d1:23:e6:b5)
    Type: IPv4 (0x0800)
▼ Internet Protocol Version 4, Src: 17.167.192.176, Dst: 192.168.43.204
    0100 .... = Version: 4
    .... 0101 = Header Length: 20 bytes
  ▶ Differentiated Services Field: 0x00 (DSCP: CS0, ECN: Not-ECT)
    Total Length: 381
    Identification: 0x34c5 (13509)
  ▶ Flags: 0x02 (Don't Fragment)
    Fragment offset: 0
    Time to live: 237
    Protocol: TCP (6)
  ▶ Header checksum: 0x98e9 [validation disabled]
    Source: 17.167.192.176
    Destination: 192.168.43.204
    [Source GeoIP: Unknown]
    [Destination GeoIP: Unknown]
▶ Transmission Control Protocol, Src Port: 443 (443), Dst Port: 49184 (49184), Seq: 4081, Ack: 184, Len: 341
▶ [4 Reassembled TCP Segments (4421 bytes): #107(1360), #109(1360), #111(1360), #112(341)]
▼ Secure Sockets Layer
  ▼ TLSv1 Record Layer: Handshake Protocol: Multiple Handshake Messages
      Content Type: Handshake (22)
      Version: TLS 1.0 (0x0301)
      Length: 4416
    ▶ Handshake Protocol: Server Hello
0000  b8 8d 12 21 1d 0e c0 bd  d1 23 e6 b5 08 00 45 00   ...!.....#....E.
0010  01 7d 34 c5 40 00 ed 06  98 e9 11 a7 c0 b0 c0 a8   .}4.@...........
0020  2b cc 01 bb c0 20 74 7b  4c 61 f5 32 1a dd 50 18   +.... t{ La.2..P.
0030  0f e9 e8 33 00 00 f8 45  01 08 01 06 08 2b 06 01   ...3...E.....+..
0040  05 05 07 03 01 06 08 2b  06 01 05 05 07 03 02 30   .......+.......0
 Frame (395 bytes)   Reassembled TCP (4421 bytes)
                                    Packets: 169 · Displayed: 169 (100.0%)   Profile: Default
```

A. The client is trying to establish a TCP handshake.

B. A Hello Server packet has been crafted.

C. The packet does not need to be fragmented.

D. The client is trying to establish an SSL connection.

Chapter

4

Practice Test 4

1. Which of the following encryption algorithms uses two large prime numbers?
   A. RSA
   B. AES
   C. El Gamal
   D. RC5

2. What can be said about asymmetric encryption?
   A. The two keys are not related mathematically.
   B. The two keys are mathematically related.
   C. Both keys do the same thing.
   D. One key is shared between both parties.

3. What protection characteristics are in use with IPsec transport mode?
   A. The header is encrypted.
   B. Both payload and message are encrypted.
   C. It provides authentication to the sender's data.
   D. It provides encryption to the payload only.

4. Which of the following defines the private, non-routable IP address ranges?
   A. RFC 1929
   B. RFC 1918
   C. NIST 1918
   D. RFC 1921

5. Which DNS record maps an IP address to a hostname?
   A. MX
   B. A
   C. AAA
   D. MR

6. In a POODLE attack, what cryptographic protocol would the victim revert back to?
   A. TLS 1.2
   B. TLS 1.0
   C. SSL 2.0
   D. SSL 3.0

7. You are a disgruntled worker who is trying to access a blocked website at your job. You attempted to use a proxy server, but the website was blocked too. You then attempt to change the URL into another format that may not be blocked by the firewall, such as binary. What are you attempting to do?
   A. URL encoding
   B. URL obfuscating

C. URL scrambling

D. URL encryption

8. During an annual security training course you are facilitating, you place a call to another employee picked randomly who is not part of the training class. In this call, you state that you work in the help desk department and request their password in order to reset an account you noticed is locked. What risk are you demonstrating?

   A. Social engineering

   B. Weak passwords

   C. Malware being installed by workers

   D. Spam emails circulating the office

9. What operating speed does IEEE 802.11g use?

   A. 10 Mbps

   B. 54 Gbps

   C. 54 Mbps

   D. 100+ Mbps

10. What key size range does RC4 use within WEP?

    A. 32 to 232 bits

    B. 16 to 40 bits

    C. 40 to 256 bits

    D. 40 to 232 bits

11. What command in Windows allows you to bring up a list of startup items and their locations in the Registry?

    A. Mslookup

    B. MSConfig

    C. Regedit

    D. `iexplorer.exe`

12. WEP's initialization vectors (IVs) are relatively small and therefore easily predictable. What other aspect makes IVs susceptible to eavesdropping?

    A. They are sent in the clear.

    B. They are not susceptible to eavesdropping.

    C. The attacker has to capture enough packets to see the IVs.

    D. The IVs use weak encryption.

13. In SQL, what input value or term means *everything*?

    A. *

    B. ALL

    C. SELECT

    D. FROM

14. As a security administrator, you are tasked with developing a technical solution to prevent scam and phishing emails from being generated by your company. What is one method you can use to perform this?

    A. Updating the employees address book on the domain

    B. Implementing digital signatures

    C. Implementing social engineering training

    D. Implementing a username and password policy for sending emails

15. In Kerberos, which ticket is presented to a server to grant access to a service?

    A. TGS

    B. KDC

    C. TGT

    D. AS

16. Which term describes how information is collected and handled in order to provide assurance that there has been no tampering or manipulation of evidence?

    A. Chain of evidence

    B. Custody of evidence

    C. Custodial of custody

    D. Chain of custody

17. As a security consultant, your customer provides you with its processes, plans, and procedures regarding how it responds to hazards and business operations disruptions. What type of documents are in your possession?

    A. Incident handling

    B. Business continuity plan

    C. Disaster recovery plan

    D. Fault tolerance capabilities

18. What port does a fraggle attack use?

    A. UDP port 7

    B. TCP port 7

    C. TCP 21

    D. TCP 53

19. What method is used to send spam or malicious content over instant messaging applications?

    A. Spim

    B. Spam

C. Ham and Cheese (HAC)

D. Phishing

20. In wireless communications, what frequency type uses all available frequencies simultaneously and in parallel?

A. Frequency hop spread spectrum

B. Orthogonal frequency-division multiplexing

C. Spread spectrum

D. Direct sequence spread spectrum

21. What type of attack is a hoax?

A. Spam

B. Social engineering

C. Whaling

D. Manipulation

22. What is the goal of having a baseline image?

A. To have an image that receives the required security packages

B. So that all workstations have the same applications

C. So the company is using the resources they paid for

D. To deploy images faster

23. What software technique tests for input values of programs and applications?

A. Fizzing

B. Fuzzing

C. Obfuscating

D. Encoding

24. If you were to lose a mobile device, what would be the appropriate response to prevent personal data and information from being recovered by an untrusted subject?

A. Encryption

B. Remote backup

C. Remote screen lock

D. Remote wipe

25. At what stage within Kerberos is the subject authenticated?

A. When the client presents the TGS ticket

B. When the client receives the TGT

C. When the client requests a ST

D. When the client accesses the resources it requested

26. As a black hat, you are targeting a sever room that contains important data. Which unconventional method would you use to DoS the entire room?

   A. Target the routers by DDoS.

   B. Conduct a fraggle attack on the servers.

   C. Target the HVAC units.

   D. Change all the administrator login information.

27. Which of the following transfers risk to a third party?

   A. Mitigation

   B. Disaster recovery plan

   C. Assigning risk

   D. None, because risk cannot be transferred

28. What is the process of collecting, protecting, conducting analysis on, and maintaining the integrity of evidence to be later used in court?

   A. Forensics

   B. Chain of custody

   C. Incident Response

   D. Incident Handling

29. Which of the following is one of the goals for incident response?

   A. To recover as quickly as possible

   B. To continue operations during the incident

   C. To maintain evidence

   D. To identify how the incident occurred

30. Which corporation developed SSL?

   A. Microsoft

   B. Netscape

   C. Google

   D. America Online

31. What is the purpose of dividing networks?

   A. To create larger networks

   B. To create more broadcast domains

   C. Ease of management

   D. Aggregate networks together

32. Which of the following RFCs includes guidelines on how to collect and archive evidence?

   A. RFC 1918

   B. RFC 3337

C. RFC 3298

D. RFC 3227

33. As a security administrator, you task your team to conduct a review to determine who has increased their user access privilege over time. What are they evaluating?

A. Privilege escalation

B. Privilege abuse

C. Privilege scope creep

D. Access right creep

34. Which of the following is the highest classification level used by the US government?

A. Top Secret

B. Secret

C. For Your Eyes Only

D. Confidential

35. Which of the following focuses on restoring an organization's business process or operation?

A. Business continuity plan

B. Creating a disaster recovery plan

C. Developing high redundancy servers

D. Reducing the availability

36. Which backup method copies only files in which the flagged archive bit is set?

A. Full

B. Differential

C. Incremental

D. Partial

37. As a black hat, you are targeting a banking firm to knock it offline. You understand that the longer the firm is down, the more money it loses. There is a set time limit on how long the firm can be offline and still recover. What time limit are you trying to exceed to bring the banking firm down?

A. Recovery point objective

B. Mean time to recover

C. Mean time to failure

D. Maximum tolerable downtime

38. Which of the following is the correct humidity level for an information system environment?

A. Below 40 percent humidity

B. Above 60 percent humidity

    C. Between 20 and 40 percent humidity

    D. Between 40 and 60 percent humidity

39. As a security administrator, you require members of the workforce and new hires to sign a document that details what is and what is not acceptable to use with regard to telephones, printers, and even computers. What policy type are you enforcing?

    A. User agreement policy

    B. Acceptable use policy

    C. Security agreement policy

    D. Computer abuse policy

40. You are a security consultant, and your customer is asking you to conduct an assessment of its disaster recovery plan. Which of the following methods would you use to recommend to update and evaluate the customer's disaster recover plan?

    A. Conducting a risk analysis and assessment

    B. Developing a business impact analysis

    C. Develop user training and awareness.

    D. Review the maintenance and assessment of the plan.

41. Which of the following is most important when it comes to incident response?

    A. Eradication

    B. Containment

    C. Analysis

    D. Detection

42. In the TCP three-way handshake, which is next after the initial SYN packet is sent?

    A. An ACK is received.

    B. A SYN is received.

    C. A SYN/ACK is sent.

    D. An ACK is sent.

43. Which of the following tools is used for war dialing?

    A. PAWS

    B. LOIC

    C. Cain & Abel

    D. Butt dialer

44. Which flag forces both sender and receiver on the network to terminate their connection with one another?

    A. FIN

    B. RST

    C. URG

    D. SYN

45. Which character means NOT when defining a Snort rule?

   A. N

   B. !

   C. #

   D. %

46. What does NTFS file streaming provide?

   A. It can hide a file behind another file.

   B. It prevents a file from being changed.

   C. It prevents a file from being moved.

   D. It prevents an unauthorized user from viewing the file.

47. Which of the following allows you to compile a source file within the C programming language?

   A. `gc+ source.c newsource.exe`

   B. `g++ source.cpp newsource.exe`

   C. `g++ source.c newsource.exe`

   D. `gcc source.c newsource.exe`

48. Which option describes the act of rummaging through trash to find important data?

   A. Dumpster swimming

   B. Social engineering

   C. Dumpster collection

   D. Dumpster diving

49. As a black hat, you forge an identification badge and dress in clothes associated with a maintenance worker. You attempt to follow other maintenance personnel as they enter the power grid facility. What are you attempting to do??

   A. Piggybacking

   B. Social engineering

   C. Tailgating

   D. Impersonating

50. Chris decides to download some music from a website while at work. When he opens the music files, a pop-up notification informs Chris that he must send $500 US dollars to a PayPal account using the email address Shoju@scorpion.ru if he wants access to his system again. What do you think Chris may have installed?

   A. Ransomware

   B. Adware

   C. Cryptoware

   D. Trojan

51. What server configuration groups them together and provides redundancy and fault tolerance?

A. Clustering

B. High availability

C. Fault tolerance

D. Server redundancy

52. What type of label is given to a subject for security reasons?

A. Classification

B. Clearance

C. Secret

D. Confidential

53. A safegaurd is a security function that provides protection. What are two factors you must consider before committing to a safeguard?

A. Cost and quantity

B. Cost and type

C. Cost and benefit

D. Technical and logical

54. Which term best describes the absence or weakness of a safeguard related to an asset?

A. Vulnerability

B. Risk

C. Exploit

D. Threat

55. You are a security administrator charged with protecting data from being emanated in your work environment. Which program would you use to align your security policies in order to prevent data from emanating?

A. TEMPEST

B. IEEE 802.11i

C. IEEE 802.1x

D. Encryption

56. What is a Faraday cage?

A. A cage that houses encryption keys

B. A cage designed to keep people out

C. A cage that blocks electromagnetic signals

D. A cage that holds backup tapes

57. On what default port(s) does SCP operate?

A. TCP port 22

B. TCP port 21

    C. TCP port 24

    D. TCP port 21 and 22

58. What is the purpose of using an extranet?

    A. To allow the public to access a company's resources

    B. To implement a business-to-business solution that functions like a DMZ

    C. To allow internal users to access DMZ resources

    D. To implement public access that functions like a DMZ

59. For an anomaly-based IPS to run optimally, what first must be determined?

    A. Updated signatures

    B. Accurate rules set

    C. Updated firmware

    D. Network baseline set

60. Which of the following attacks uses UDP packets to target the broadcast address and cause a DDoS?

    A. Smurf

    B. Fraggle

    C. Land

    D. Teardrop

61. Which tool causes sockets to be used up and can cause services to freeze or crash?

    A. LOIC

    B. Slowloris

    C. Cain & Abel

    D. John the Ripper

62. Which of the following takes advantage of a threat?

    A. Threat actor

    B. Threat agent

    C. Threat vector

    D. Threat object

63. What is a user or administrator who has access to an information system called?

    A. Cyber persona

    B. Object

    C. Subject

    D. User profile

64. What is a computing platform with a software solution that is based on the cloud or on a virtual stack for customers to use?

    A. Platform as a service

    B. Software as service

C. FTP

D. Web application

65. What is the act of looking over the shoulder of a victim to capture the information being displayed on their machine?

   A. Piggybacking

   B. Impersonation

   C. Shoulder surfing

   D. Shoulder peering

66. Which protocol does IPsec support natively?

   A. IPv4

   B. IPv6

   C. IPX

   D. AppleTalk

67. Which of the following uses sockets that are unique to a web connection and translate from private to public and vice versa?

   A. NAT

   B. IPsec

   C. PAT

   D. Proxy

68. Which of the following allows networks to be subnetted into various sizes?

   A. NAT

   B. CIDR

   C. OSPF

   D. BGP

69. As a network administrator, you are tasked to separate different networks in order to increase security. By doing so, you attempt to create networks for users with a "need to know" policy. What can you do to ensure that only the workstations for those users participate in those layer 2 networks?

   A. Create broadcast multiple domains.

   B. Create VLANs.

   C. Maintain the collision domains.

   D. Implement a VPN solution.

70. At what layer does ICMP operate?

   A. Layer 2

   B. Layer 3

   C. Layer 5

   D. Layer 4

71. What is the best solution for making a backup copy of a system?

   A. Full backup

   B. Bit-level image

   C. Incremental

   D. Differential

72. Which of the following is the best defense against a zero day attack?

   A. User awareness training

   B. Up-to-date patches applied

   C. Removing applications that are not required

   D. Keeping up to date with firewall rules

73. Which type of network uses a group of zombie computers to carry out the commands of the bot master?

   A. Zombie net

   B. Zombie group

   C. Botnet

   D. Bot heard

74. Which of the following Trojan port numbers are associated with the SniperNet?

   A. 666

   B. 1807

   C. 2366

   D. 667

75. What is the main purpose of installing a Trojan?

   A. To cause a DoS on a computer

   B. To delete files on a computer

   C. To encrypt the system

   D. To establish a covert connection

76. Which of the following applications allows you to crack WEP passwords in a wireless network?

   A. Cain & Abel

   B. Wireshark

   C. Traceroute

   D. John the Ripper

77. Which protocol extension does Heartbleed take advantage of?

    A. Heartbeat

    B. X.509

    C. OpenSSL

    D. TLS

78. Other than disabling SSL 3.0, what options are available to prevent the POODLE exploit from being effective?

    A. Updating the workstation firmware

    B. Disabling the CBC mode cipher in SSL

    C. Switching to the Mozilla Firefox or Google Chrome web browser

    D. Downgrading to SSL 2.0

79. Fences, security cameras, and armed guards are considered what type of control?

    A. Physical

    B. Technical

    C. Logical

    D. Operational

80. Which of the following Trojans use TCP 666?

    A. TCP Wrapper

    B. Tini

    C. Wormhole

    D. Doom

81. Which of the following devices allows a black hat to collect all the data traffic with minimal effort?

    A. Layer 2 switch

    B. Bridge

    C. Router

    D. Hub

82. Which of the following describes a network appliance that acts as an intermediary server?

    A. Stateful firewall

    B. Packet filter firewall

    C. Proxy firewall

    D. Data server

83. Which of the following is considered a natural event?

    A. Lightning strike

    B. Malware

    C. Data corruption

    D. Electrical fire

84. What must the digital signature authority have to validate a message?

    A. User's digital signature

    B. User's private key

    C. The original message

    D. The hash value

85. Which of the following algorithms successfully implemented the public key cryptosystem?

    A. AES

    B. El Gammal

    C. Diffie-Hellman

    D. RSA

86. Which of the following attacks forges a TCP packet as both the source and destination IP address of the victim and causes the vicitm's computer to freeze or crash?

    A. Land

    B. Fraggle

    C. Teardrop

    D. Smurf

87. What is the third portion of the TCP header field that comes after source port and destination port?

    A. RESV

    B. WINDOW

    C. SEQ NUMBER

    D. ACK NUMBER

88. A message that carries data and acknowledgments is called what?

    A. Segments

    B. Packets

    C. Frames

    D. Nibbles

89. You are a black hat who was successful in sending out malicious emails from one of the workers at a card game factory. The malware in the digitally signed email spread quickly, and most users were actually surprised that the victim was capable of doing such a terrible thing. What two things must you have in order to carry out the digitally signed email attack?

    A. Username and password

    B. Token and PIN

    C. Username and token

    D. Token and access to computer

90. Which of the following is considered an AAA server?

    A. Kerberos

    B. Solaris

    C. Apache

    D. Exchange

91. What is a stack pointer within memory?

    A. It points to the next memory pointer in the stack.

    B. It points at the bottom of the stack.

    C. Memory does not use a stack pointer.

    D. It points at the top of the stack.

92. Apache OpenOffice and Microsoft Office have a built-in feature that allows the user to automate a series of specified commands. These commands usually assist with daily routine tasks. This feature can be used in conjunction with launching malware. What feature is this?

    A. File sharing services

    B. Object Link

    C. Macro

    D. Compression

93. In virus scanning, what is the telltale sign of a virus?

    A. Hash value

    B. Signature

    C. Definition

    D. Trojan

94. When a security administrator is trying to reduce physical access to the backup vault, what type of control will they implement?

    A. Physical control

    B. Technical control

    C. Administrative control

    D. Logical control

95. As a white hat, you are hired to conduct an assessment of a target web server. After you conduct your assessment, you provide your client with your findings and recommendations to improve the security posture. What did you formally hand over to your client?

    A. Problem tracker

    B. Fix action plan

   C. Vulnerability list

   D. Risk mitigation plan

96. As a black hat, you use ToneLoc to dial random numbers in order to connect to a modem that is providing service to a server. What type of attack are you conducting?

   A. Wardriving

   B. DoS

   C. Scanning

   D. War dialing

97. In Linux, how would you create a new user in a terminal?

   A. `# useradd /home/samarea ssamarea`

   B. `>useradd raeleah`

   C. `cuser ray_j /home/ray_j`

   D. `useradd savion`

98. In Linux, what method uses a brute-force effort to locate a file?

   A. `find`

   B. `grep`

   C. `|`

   D. `search`

99. Besides usernames and passwords, what other critical objects can be retrieved by using Hearbleed?

   A. Tokens

   B. X.509

   C. X.35

   D. Symmetric keys

100. As a white hat, your customer asks what type of assessments you can conduct. What are they?

   A. Risk, threat, and vulnerability

   B. Malware, risk, and exploit

   C. Risk, vulnerability, and exploits

   D. Risk, mitigation, and vulnerability

101. A method that defends against a flooding attack and massive DoS attacks is referred to as what?

   A. Defense in depth

   B. Spam blocker

   C. Flood safe

   D. Flood guard

102. A firewall that blocks all traffic by default is known as what?

    A. Implicit allow

    B. Implicit deny

    C. Deny all

    D. Implicit prevent all

103. On which UPD ports does SNMP operate?

    A. 53

    B. 160 and 161

    C. 161 and 162

    D. 167

104. In IPsec, what is known as the security association manager?

    A. IKE

    B. ISAKMP

    C. VPN

    D. ESP

105. In WPA2, what AAA server can be used in the enterprise configuration?

    A. RADIUS

    B. Exchange

    C. Solaris

    D. Netware

106. The act of falsifying data is also known as what?

    A. Boink

    B. Packet crafting

    C. Spoofing

    D. Data diddling

107. When a black hat sends corrupted UDP packets to port 53, it can cause a Windows system to crash. What attack is the adversary trying to conduct?

    A. Bonk

    B. Boink

    C. Ping flood

    D. DNS poison

108. As a black hat, you are injecting inputs into the back of the LDAP server instead of the database. What are you trying to conduct?

    A. SQL injection

    B. X.25 injection

    C. LDAP injection

    D. LDAP fuzzing

109. Which of the following allows the adversary to jump from the web directory to another part of the file system?

    A. Directory traversal

    B. Pivoting

    C. Directory hopping

    D. Directory shifting

110. When applications create variable memory segments in a dynamic fashion, what type of memory is being used?

    A. Stack

    B. Heap

    C. Virtual memory

    D. Virtual stack

111. As part of hardening a server, which of the following would the administrator want to configure prior to putting it into the DMZ?

    A. Disable unnecessary ports.

    B. Open all ports.

    C. Disable all accounts.

    D. Reducing file restrictions

112. When inputting data into the data payload field of a SYN packet, what is the adversary trying to do?

    A. Packet crafting

    B. Data injection

    C. Session crafting

    D. Fragmentation

113. What is a unique identifier that is used in Snort?

    A. SID

    B. ID

    C. PID

    D. NID

114. Which of the fooling tools can be used to steal cookies between a client and a server to use in a replay attack?

    A. Mouse

    B. Ferret

    C. Ratpack

    D. Nezumi

115. Which option describes the architecture in the following image?

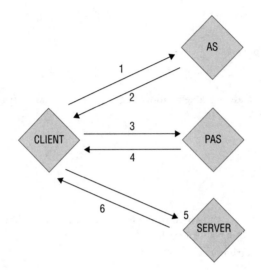

    A. Kerberos

    B. SESAME

    C. TACACS

    D. RADIUS

116. What type of operation is being conducted in the following image?

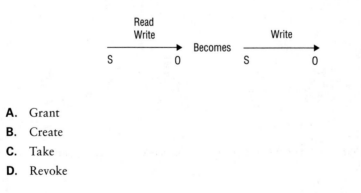

    A. Grant

    B. Create

    C. Take

    D. Revoke

117. What is missing from the following diagram?

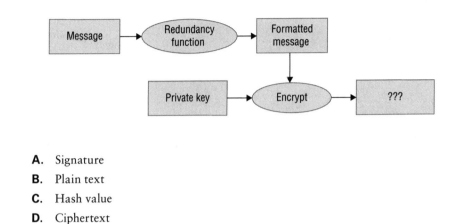

   A. Signature

   B. Plain text

   C. Hash value

   D. Ciphertext

118. What is missing from the following diagram?

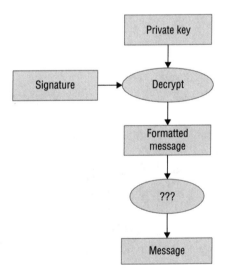

   A. Verification

   B. Hashed value

   C. Digital signature

   D. Public key Encrypting

119. What would be the results of this XOR?

	1	0	0	1	1	1	0	1
XOR	1	1	0	0	0	1	0	1

- **A.** 01011000
- **B.** 10100101
- **C.** 10100111
- **D.** 10010100

120. What type of cipher is being depicted in the following image?

```
ABCDEFGHIJKLMNOPQRSTUVWXYZ
POULKJHMINBVYTREWQGFDSACXZ
```

- **A.** Caesar cipher
- **B.** Polyalphabetic cipher
- **C.** Monalphabetic cipher
- **D.** One-time key pad

121. What is the name of the pointer that is missing in the following diagram?

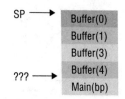

- **A.** SP
- **B.** HP
- **C.** MP
- **D.** BP

122. In the following screen shot, what sequence completes the three-way handshake with 23.253.184.229?

No.	Time	Source	Destination	Protocol	Length	Info
1	0…	Apple_21:1d:0e	Broadcast	ARP	42	Who has 192.168.1.1? Tell 192.168.1.118
2	0…	Netgear_39:0d:8f	Apple_21:1d:0e	ARP	42	192.168.1.1 is at 84:1b:5e:39:0d:8f
3	0…	192.168.1.118	192.168.1.1	DNS	83	Standard query 0x8c29 A community.allhiphop.com
4	0…	192.168.1.1	192.168.1.118	DNS	186	Standard query response 0x8c29 A community.allhiphop…
5	0…	192.168.1.118	23.253.184.229	TCP	78	50204 → 80 [SYN] Seq=0 Win=65535 Len=0 MSS=1460 WS=32…
6	0…	192.168.1.118	23.253.184.229	TCP	78	50205 → 80 [SYN] Seq=0 Win=65535 Len=0 MSS=1460 WS=32…
7	0…	23.253.184.229	192.168.1.118	TCP	74	80 → 50204 [SYN, ACK] Seq=0 Ack=1 Win=4140 Len=0 MSS=…
8	0…	192.168.1.118	23.253.184.229	TCP	66	50204 → 80 [ACK] Seq=1 Ack=1 Win=65535 Len=0 TSval=37…
9	0…	23.253.184.229	192.168.1.118	TCP	74	80 → 50205 [SYN, ACK] Seq=0 Ack=1 Win=4140 Len=0 MSS=…
10	0…	192.168.1.118	23.253.184.229	TCP	66	50205 → 80 [ACK] Seq=1 Ack=1 Win=65535 Len=0 TSval=37…
11	0…	192.168.1.118	192.168.1.1	DNS	76	Standard query 0x6be3 A depositfiles.com
12	0…	192.168.1.1	192.168.1.118	DNS	268	Standard query response 0x6be3 A depositfiles.com A 9…
13	0…	192.168.1.118	94.242.227.163	TCP	78	50206 → 80 [SYN] Seq=0 Win=65535 Len=0 MSS=1460 WS=32…
14	0…	94.242.227.163	192.168.1.118	TCP	74	80 → 50206 [SYN, ACK] Seq=0 Ack=1 Win=33304 Len=0 SAC…
15	0…	192.168.1.118	94.242.227.163	TCP	66	50206 → 80 [ACK] Seq=1 Ack=1 Win=131744 Len=0 TSval=3…
16	1…	192.168.1.118	192.168.1.1	DNS	73	Standard query 0x5d88 A www.yahoo.com

> Frame 1: 42 bytes on wire (336 bits), 42 bytes captured (336 bits) on interface 0
> Ethernet II, Src: Apple_21:1d:0e (b8:8d:12:21:1d:0e), Dst: Broadcast (ff:ff:ff:ff:ff:ff)
> Address Resolution Protocol (request)

```
0000  ff ff ff ff ff ff b8 8d  12 21 1d 0e 08 06 00 01   ........ .!......
0010  08 00 06 04 00 01 b8 8d  12 21 1d 0e c0 a8 01 76   ........ .!.....v
0020  00 00 00 00 00 00 c0 a8  01 01                     ........ ..
```

Packets: 1653 · Displayed: 1653 (100.0%)   Profile: Default

A. 5025

B. 1

C. 74

D. 64

123. In the following screen shot, what flag is set on frame 57523?

- **A.** 0x02
- **B.** 0x00
- **C.** 0x01
- **D.** 0x20

124. In the following screen shot, what is the plaintext password that was used to create the secured web connection by the client?

A. @wERy%9q>[cAF{A7>}rQMV8@=b

B. The key cannot be derived.

C. 0x0303

D. b99d4098d877458052b57910abb78b259a9b

125. As seen in the following screen shot, is the current connection vulnerable to Heartbleed?

A. No. Heart bleed affects TLS 1.0.1 to 1.0.1f.

B. No. Heart bleed affects only SSL 3.0.

C. There is not enough information to tell.

D. Heart bleed is not the vulnerability; it is a heartbeat.

Chapter

5

Practice Test 5

1. When a black hat is querying for a number of services or login information on a target system, what are they trying to accomplish?

   A. Enumeration

   B. Scanning

   C. Footprinting

   D. Fingerprinting

2. Which of the following allows the adversary to obtain passwords online in a passive manner?

   A. Sniffing

   B. Man in the middle

   C. Password cracking

   D. Account creation

3. Which of the following passwords will take the most effort to crack?

   A. P@$$w0rd

   B. Pass123

   C. $@($)!_

   D. Thisismypasswordandnoonecanstealit

4. Where is the event log located in Linux OS?

   A. /home/log

   B. /var/log

   C. /log/

   D. /home/system32/log

5. In Linux, which of the following accounts denotes the administrator?

   A. Admin

   B. Administrator

   C. root

   D. su

6. Which of the following is another name for NAT overload?

   A. PAT

   B. NAT+

   C. NAT port

   D. PAT overload

7. Which of the following is part of the overall portion of the SID?

   A. UID

   B. RID

   C. USD

   D. L5R

8. What is accomplished by a combination of ping sweeping and enumerating a target?

   A. Fingerprinting

   B. Footprinting

   C. Reconnaissance

   D. Identification

9. What response time measurement is used by default within the tracert program?

   A. Seconds

   B. Milliseconds

   C. Minutes

   D. None

10. What is the encryption key length in DES?

   A. 64

   B. 128

   C. 56

   D. 128

11. Which of the following encryption ciphers replaced DES and was renamed AES?

   A. RSA

   B. AES

   C. Rijndael

   D. RC5

12. What completes the three-way handshake in the TCP connection?

   A. RST

   B. SYN/ACK

   C. ACK

   D. FIN

13. Using XOR, which of the following outputs a value of 1?

   A. 0 + 1

   B. 1 and 1

   C. 0 and 0

   D. 1 and 0

14. Which of the following outlaws the unauthorized or unsolicited act of taking control over a system that is not yours?

   A. PATRIOT Act

   B. SPY Act

   C. FISMA Act

   D. FoIA

15. Which of the following allows you to quickly search for websites that are vulnerable to SQL injections?

   A. Google Dorks

   B. Bing Hacks

   C. Tracert

   D. 1=1'

16. What is the size of each of the fields in a UDP header?

   A. 16 bits

   B. 32 bits

   C. 8 bytes

   D. 16 bytes

17. The second administrator that is under a Windows system has the RID of what?

   A. Not a RID, but a SID of 502

   B. RID 501

   C. RID 1001

   D. RID 1000

18. When trying to identify all the workstations on a subnet, what method might you choose?

   A. Port scan

   B. Anonymizer

   C. Ping sweep

   D. Web crawler

19. What is the default port used for DNS?

   A. 80

   B. 22

   C. 8080

   D. 53

20. Which of the following tools can be used to crack passwords ?

   A. Cain & Abel

   B. ToneLoc

   C. Wireshark

   D. WarVOX

21. Which connection type is considered a half-open connection?

   A. FIN

   B. SYN

   C. SYN/ACK

   D. URG

22. Which tool can be used to query DNS?

   A. Twofish

   B. Cain & Abel

   C. WarVOX

   D. Dig

23. Using Snort, which rule type allows for notification only if there is a match?

   A. Drop

   B. Alert

   C. Pass

   D. Bing

24. Which switch in Nmap allows for a full TCP connect scan?

   A. -sS

   B. -sU

   C. -FC

   D. -sT

25. What type of control is a firewall?

   A. Barrier

   B. Administrator

   C. Logical

   D. Physical

26. Which of the following denotes the root directory in Linux OS?

   A. \

   B. /

   C. C:\

   D. root/

27. As a black hat, you call into the city manager's office claiming to be a part of the help desk team. You ask the clerk for her username and password to install the latest Microsoft Office suite. What type of attack are you conducting?

   A. Impersonation

   B. Piggybacking

   C. Masquerading

   D. Tailgating

28. As a black hat, you are driving in your vehicle looking for wireless access points to connect to. What type of attack are you conducting?

   A. War dialing

   B. Drive-by scanning

   C. War chalking

   D. Wardriving

29. What is the process called when you're trying to inject bogus entries into the ARP table?

   A. Enumeration

   B. RARP

   C. ARP poisoning

   D. L2 dumping

30. What is the maximum input for a Windows login field?

   A. 16

   B. 127

   C. 256

   D. 32

31. A black hat was able to install a device at an unattended workstation and was able to recover passwords, account information, and other information the next day. What did the black hat install?

   A. Keylogger

   B. Key scanner

   C. Rootkit

   D. Trojan

32. What command displays the network configuration in Linux OS?

   A. `ipconfig`

   B. `netstat`

   C. `ls`

   D. `ifconfig`

33. What directory holds the basic commands in the Linux OS?

   A. `/etc`

   B. `/bin`

   C. `/`

   D. `/config`

34. A black hat is dressed as a postal worker. Holding some large boxes, he follows a group of workers to make his drop-off in the back of the facility. What is the black hat trying to conduct?

   A. Tailgating

   B. Sliding

   C. Piggybacking

   D. Shimming

35. What system element is used to store information and is installed by the web server?

    A. A text file

    B. Cookies

    C. HTML file

    D. XML file

36. You are walking around downtown picking up on open wireless access points. As you identify these access points, you place a symbol on a nearby building. What activity are you conducting?

    A. War walking

    B. Wardriving

    C. Footprinting

    D. War chalking

37. What type of virus can change or rewrite itself every time it infects a new file?

    A. Polymorphic virus

    B. Metamorphic virus

    C. Trojan virus

    D. Shell virus

38. Which hashing algorithm was developed by the NSA and has a 160-bit output?

    A. MD5

    B. HAVAL

    C. DSA

    D. SHA-1

39. Aside from port 80, what is another common port used to connect to a web server?

    A. 8080

    B. 21

    C. 54

    D. 110

40. Which Nmap switch utilizes the slowest scan?

    A. -T

    B. -sT

    C. -s0

    D. -sX

41. Which of the following applications is used to inspect packets?

    A. Wireshark

    B. Cain & Abel

   C. Aircrack

   D. Nmap

42. Which process defines the act of an adversary copying an entire website to be used for subsequent attacks?

   A. Web copy

   B. Web crawling

   C. Web caching

   D. Web dump

43. How would an administrator set a password for a user in Linux?

   A. `password user pass123`

   B. `chmod pass user pass123`

   C. `pass user pass123`

   D. `passwd user pass123`

44. In Windows, what is the command to display the ARP cache?

   A. `ifconfig /-a`

   B. `arp -a`

   C. `-a arp`

   D. `ipconfig /arp -a`

45. Which application can provide DNS zone transfer information?

   A. Cain & Abel

   B. ICMP

   C. Nslookup

   D. Domain Name Service

46. Which of the following signifies the parent domain of a DNS Server?

   A. `myserver.com`

   B. `.com`

   C. `http://myserver.com`

   D. `http://www.myserver.com`

47. Which is the second phase in the ethical hacking methodology?

   A. Reconnaissance

   B. Maintaining access

   C. Covering your tracks

   D. Scanning and enumeration

48. What system uses a certificate authority?

   A. Realm

   B. SESAME

    C. PKI

    D. ICY Manipulator

49. Which site can you use to view a collection of vulnerabilities?

    A. `nvd.nist.gov`

    B. `google.com`

    C. `hackmybox.net`

    D. `breachthedoor.org`

50. As a business analyst, you study and collect information about your competitor using Google and the competitor's website and products. Which of the following best defines the actions you are performing?

    A. Google hacking

    B. Espionage

    C. Competitive intelligence

    D. Tradecraft

51. Which of the following relies on plaintext transmission when sending community strings as a means of authentication?

    A. SFTP

    B. SNMPv3

    C. SNMPv1

    D. Telnet

52. Which of the following is a capability that can be used with WPA2?

    A. RADIUS

    B. SESAME

    C. PKI

    D. Kerberos

53. A bank teller must have authorization with the bank manager to withdraw a large sum of money for the bank customer. Without the manager, she cannot accomplish the task. What access control is being performed in this scenario?

    A. Job rotation

    B. Separation of duties

    C. Multifactor

    D. Type 1 control

54. For a threat to be exploited, what must be identified first?

    A. Threat vector

    B. Malware

    C. A vulnerability

    D. A threat surface

55. As a black hat, you were successful in capturing credentials of your neighbor's web session to their bank account by sniffing their wireless connection. You were able to log in to their account and deposit their funds into your account. What attack type did you perform?

    A. Replay attack

    B. Denial of service

    C. Credential harvesting

    D. Land attack

56. In order for a wireless client to connect to an access point to gain access or be challenged with authentication, what information must be known?

    A. Key

    B. Username and password

    C. X.509 certificate

    D. SSID

57. What must a user have in order to sniff wireless traffic?

    A. Wireless device set to promiscuous mode

    B. Wireless device that has 2.4 GHz and 5 GHz set to read only

    C. Wireshark

    D. Ettercap set to clone

58. What command within the Linux OS can be used to delete files from a directory?

    A. del

    B. er

    C. -rm

    D. rm

59. Your company has been targeted by a series of phishing emails. In order to deter the attack, you quickly tell your users to verify senders. How do you go about implementing this?

    A. Ensure that the email is digitally signed.

    B. Call the sender and verify.

    C. Ensure that the email was not encrypted.

    D. Reply back to their message and ask for their public key.

60. What type of control should be used to grant the right access to users?

    A. Psychical

    B. Operational

    C. Technical

    D. Logical

61. What type of malware can be used to provide backdoor access to a system?

   A. Trojan

   B. Rootkit

   C. Root virus

   D. Spyware

62. Which type of software is considered a framework, a set of preinstalled tools, that aids in compromising and exploiting targeted systems?

   A. Cain & Abel

   B. Metasploit

   C. Mutavault

   D. Ettercap

63. What sets up a null session using Windows?

   A. `ftp ://yourdomain.com`

   B. `C$ \\yourdomain.com`

   C. `net use \\yourdomain\ipc$ "" /u: ""`

   D. `netcat yourdomain`

64. Taking binary code and changing it into an ASCII string can be accomplished using what method?

   A. Encoding to ASCII version 2

   B. Hashing into MD5 or SHA-1

   C. Using Base64 encoding

   D. Converting to XML format

65. A city clerk received an email asking to donate money to a charity group that operates in Nigeria. The email instructs the clerk to provide bank account information that will be used to deduct two dollars from the clerk's account every month. What may be the issue here?

   A. Spear phishing

   B. Theft

   C. Whaling

   D. Tradecraft

66. Which of the following can be used to check for wireless signals?

   A. AirCheck

   B. Netcheck

   C. Ncat

   D. AirWare

67. Which switch in Nmap allows the user to perform a fast scan?
    - **A.** -oX
    - **B.** -PT
    - **C.** -T4
    - **D.** -sS

68. A flag that is set to allow a packet to be sent out of band is considered what?
    - **A.** URG
    - **B.** FIN
    - **C.** SYN
    - **D.** PSH

69. A user who is scanning for a network size of 128 nodes would use what CIDR?
    - **A.** /24
    - **B.** /25
    - **C.** /28
    - **D.** /30

70. A black hat uses a search engine to locate websites that are possibly vulnerable to SQL injections. What search engine would they most likely be using?
    - **A.** Bing
    - **B.** Yahoo
    - **C.** Google
    - **D.** Whoami

71. A supervisor suspects that there are fraudulent activities being conducted in the workplace. What option can the supervisor employ to confirm their suspicion?
    - **A.** Duty rotation
    - **B.** Forced vacation
    - **C.** Installation of spy cameras
    - **D.** Installation of spy equipment

72. If a user wants to send information securely to another user in an open environment, what method would they use?
    - **A.** The receiver's shared key
    - **B.** The receiver's pre-shared key
    - **C.** The receiver's public key
    - **D.** The receiver's private key

73. Which record indicates the mapping of an IP address to a hostname?
    - **A.** MX
    - **B.** PTR

    C. NS

    D. CNAME

74. Which value is used in association with firewalking?

    A. TTL

    B. TCP

    C. ICMP

    D. Max hop count

75. A user side-loaded a popular app from an unauthorized third-party app store. When the user installed the app, it displayed a screen asking for payment and stating that if the payment was not received, the user would lose all access to data that was stored on their phone. What was installed on the user's phone?

    A. Trojan

    B. Spyware

    C. Malware

    D. Ransomware

76. Which camera lens provides the best support when it is used outside?

    A. Fixed lens

    B. Zoom lens

    C. Autofocus lens

    D. Auto iris lens

77. Which of the following is considered open-source information?

    A. Newspaper

    B. Trade secrets

    C. Information obtained from dumpster diving

    D. Information obtained from a man-in-the-middle attack

78. A manager routinely shifts personnel around in order to deter fraudulent activities at the job site. What protective measure is the supervisor using?

    A. Spear phishing

    B. Force vacation

    C. Duty rotation

    D. Cross training

79. Which method would allow the administrator to reduce the threat of DNS poisoning?

    A. Increase refresh time rate.

    B. Statically assign DNS entries.

    C. Remove DNS entries.

    D. Remove refresh time rate.

80. Which Google hack allows the user to search for file types that are located within a website?

    A. filetype:

    B. inurl:

    C. typefile:

    D. file:

81. Which hash algorithm produces a 160-bit value?

    A. MD5

    B. SHA-1

    C. MD6

    D. Diffie-Hellman

82. What standard format is used with certificate authorities?

    A. X.509

    B. X.500

    C. 802.1x

    D. PKI

83. In which method are two keys that are mathematically related used?

    A. Symmetric encryption

    B. Pre-shared keys

    C. Asymmetric encryption

    D. Shared keys

84. What key is included on a digital certificate?

    A. The public key is stored on the certificate.

    B. The private key is stored on the certificate.

    C. The key is not stored on the certificate.

    D. Both the public and private keys are stored on the certificate.

85. A black hat retrieved all the personal identification numbers that were used on an ATM machine. What did the black hat install?

    A. Malware

    B. Virus

    C. Keylogger

    D. Key retriever

86. Which flag will receive an RST response only if the port is closed?

    A. ACK

    B. XMAS

    C. NULL

    D. SYN

87. What is the default port used in POP3?

    A. 110

    B. 53

    C. 443

    D. 125

88. What protocol uses a back-off timer when listening on the network?

    A. CSMA/CA

    B. 802.11

    C. 802.1x

    D. CSMA/CD

89. Which of the following has the best chance of illuminating the latest attacks on a network?

    A. Signature-based IDS

    B. Packet-based IDS

    C. Behavior-based IDS

    D. Rule-based IDS

90. If you were to ARP poison the default gateway, what would be the expected results?

    A. You will receive traffic on that specific virtual local area network.

    B. You will receive all the traffic on the current network associated with the gateway.

    C. You will not receive any traffic.

    D. You may cause a DoS on the network.

91. Which of the following prevents a vehicle from ramming into a building?

    A. Bollards

    B. A fence with triple-strand razor wire

    C. Armed guards

    D. Gates

92. Which of the following AAA servers provides asymmetric encryption?

    A. Kerberos

    B. RADIUS

    C. SESAME

    D. FTP

93. Which of the following tools allows a user to monitor network activity?

    A. Cain & Abel

    B. Metasploit

    C. Wireshark

    D. Netcraft

94. What is the default command port for FTP?

    A. 22

    B. 21

    C. 20

    D. 23

95. Which of the following are not objects in Active Directory?

    A. Users

    B. Computers

    C. Printers

    D. Files

96. Which of the following tools allows the adversary to conduct phishing attacks?

    A. Social Engineering

    B. Ettercap

    C. Mimikatz

    D. Netcat

97. What tool would a black hat use to create multiple scripts that can evade detection by an IDS?

    A. ADmutate

    B. Mimikatz

    C. Cain & Abel

    D. Bluecross

98. Which of the following will inform the user that the port is closed by the client itself?

    A. ICMP Type 3, Code 3

    B. ICMP Type 3

    C. ICMP Type 1, Code 1

    D. ICMP Type 3, Code 2

99. Which of the following layers in the OSI model contains the Transport layer in the TCP/IP model?

    A. Session and Transport

    B. Transport

    C. Network and Transport

    D. Data and Network

100. Which of the following encapsulates the header and the trailer?

    A. Data-Link layer

    B. Transport layer

    C. Application layer

    D. Data-Link layer with the logical link controller set

101. What program can be used to discover firewalls?

    A. Metasploit

    B. Traceroute

    C. Nslookup

    D. Dig

102. Which of the following has no flags set and does not respond if a port is open?

    A. XMAS scan

    B. NULL scan

    C. Half-open connection

    D. ACK scan

103. Which of the following aids in fingerprinting a machine?

    A. Port sweep

    B. Nslookup

    C. Dig

    D. The -sF switch in Nmap

104. Which DNS record type provides the port and services the server is hosting?

    A. SRV

    B. PTR

    C. SVR

    D. A

105. To establish a TCP connection, what must be sent first?

    A. ACK

    B. Hello packet

    C. Broadcast packet

    D. SYN

106. An X.509 certificate uses what value to uniquely identify it?

    A. Authentication number

    B. Serial number

    C. Private key

    D. Public key

107. Which encryption algorithm uses two large prime numbers factored together?

    A. El Gammal

    B. Diffie-Hellman

    C. RSA

    D. AES

108. Which is the initial value of the SID that is used to annotate an administrator's account?

    A. 500

    B. 100

    C. 5000

    D. 1

109. Which is the last step of the CEH hacking methodology?

    A. Maintain access.

    B. Cover your tracks.

    C. Scrub the logs.

    D. Corrupt data.

110. What file within the Linux OS contains administrative information about a user?

    A. `/etc/shadow`

    B. `/etc/passwd`

    C. `/home`

    D. `/home/profile`

111. What port number is used by NetBIOS for name services?

    A. UDP port 137

    B. TCP port 137

    C. UDP port 190

    D. None

112. Which of the following rule type allows for logs and alerts in Snort?

    A. Drop

    B. Pass

    C. Alert

    D. Block

113. Which port or ports is/are affiliated with Back Orifice?

    A. 31337

    B. 2132

    C. 666

    D. 666 and 999

114. Which utility will display active network connections on a host?

 A. Netcat

 B. Netstat

 C. Nmap

 D. Ns

115. What flag(s) is set in the following screen shot?

 A. FIN

 B. ACK, FIN

 C. ACK

 D. None

116. As shown in the following screen shot, what destination port is the current TLS connection being associated with?

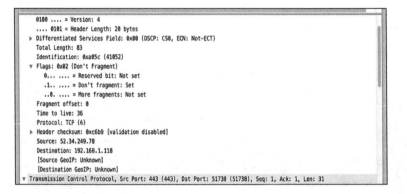

A. 51738

B. 443

C. 0101

D. Not enough information available

117. What port is stackoverflow connected with in the following screen shot?

A. 42024

B. 520303

C. 52017

D. 52020

118. As shown in the following screen shot, what is the TTL value?

```
●  ●  ●                    ⌂ rblockmon — bash — 80×24
Rays-MBP:~ rblockmon$ ping stackoverflow.com
PING stackoverflow.com (104.16.34.249): 56 data bytes
64 bytes from 104.16.34.249: icmp_seq=0 ttl=57 time=110.611 ms
64 bytes from 104.16.34.249: icmp_seq=1 ttl=57 time=23.498 ms
64 bytes from 104.16.34.249: icmp_seq=2 ttl=57 time=23.692 ms
64 bytes from 104.16.34.249: icmp_seq=3 ttl=57 time=23.303 ms
64 bytes from 104.16.34.249: icmp_seq=4 ttl=57 time=22.656 ms
64 bytes from 104.16.34.249: icmp_seq=5 ttl=57 time=24.136 ms
64 bytes from 104.16.34.249: icmp_seq=6 ttl=57 time=20.604 ms
64 bytes from 104.16.34.249: icmp_seq=7 ttl=57 time=23.487 ms
64 bytes from 104.16.34.249: icmp_seq=8 ttl=57 time=23.154 ms
64 bytes from 104.16.34.249: icmp_seq=9 ttl=57 time=23.145 ms
64 bytes from 104.16.34.249: icmp_seq=10 ttl=57 time=23.125 ms
64 bytes from 104.16.34.249: icmp_seq=11 ttl=57 time=100.855 ms
64 bytes from 104.16.34.249: icmp_seq=12 ttl=57 time=22.019 ms
^C
--- stackoverflow.com ping statistics ---
13 packets transmitted, 13 packets received, 0.0% packet loss
round-trip min/avg/max/stddev = 20.604/35.714/110.611/29.929 ms
Rays-MBP:~ rblockmon$ 
```

A. 128

B. 58

C. 64

D. 57

119. As shown in the following screen shot, at what hop did the user potentially encounter a firewall?

```
●  ●  ●                    ⌂ rblockmon — bash — 80×24
ms
 4  user-24-96-198-18.knology.net (24.96.198.18)  17.599 ms  10.577 ms  9.542 ms
 5  user-24-96-35-34.knology.net (24.96.35.34)  9.823 ms  10.642 ms  11.120 ms
 6  user-24-96-153-14.knology.net (24.96.153.14)  20.505 ms  28.997 ms  20.733 m
s
 7  dynamic-75-76-35-15.knology.net (75.76.35.15)  20.795 ms  21.908 ms  22.732
ms
 8  dynamic-75-76-35-73.knology.net (75.76.35.73)  27.340 ms  70.911 ms  26.862
ms
 9  de-cix.pat2.nyc.yahoo.com (206.130.10.78)  27.141 ms  26.498 ms  26.995 ms
10  ae-2.pat2.bfz.yahoo.com (216.115.100.74)  39.458 ms  39.941 ms
    ae-5.pat1.bfz.yahoo.com (216.115.96.65)  39.050 ms
11  et-0-0-1.msr1.bf1.yahoo.com (74.6.227.131)  34.942 ms
    et-19-1-0.msr1.bf2.yahoo.com (74.6.227.147)  37.867 ms
    et-19-1-0.msr1.bf1.yahoo.com (74.6.227.133)  37.238 ms
12  et-0-1-0.clr2-a-gdc.bf1.yahoo.com (74.6.122.17)  37.536 ms
    et-19-0-1.clr2-a-gdc.bf1.yahoo.com (74.6.122.39)  37.356 ms
    et-0-1-0.clr2-a-gdc.bf1.yahoo.com (74.6.122.17)  38.292 ms
13  po8.fab7-1-gdc.bf1.yahoo.com (72.30.22.45)  35.027 ms
    po8.fab1-1-gdc.bf1.yahoo.com (72.30.22.33)  43.781 ms
    po7.fab3-1-gdc.bf1.yahoo.com (72.30.22.5)  38.088 ms
14  po-12.bas2-7-prd.bf1.yahoo.com (98.139.129.195)  58.967 ms  42.345 ms
    po-16.bas1-7-prd.bf1.yahoo.com (98.139.130.1)  36.660 ms
15  * * *
```

A. 10

B. 14

C. 15

D. 19

120. What is the source address being used in the terminal output shown in the following screen shot?

```
● ● ●                    ⌂ rblockmon — bash — 80×24
traceroute: Warning: google.com has multiple addresses; using 74.125.21.113
traceroute to google.com (74.125.21.113), 64 hops max, 52 byte packets
 1  dd-wrt (192.168.1.1)  1.262 ms  0.806 ms  0.658 ms
 2  dynamic-24-42-128-1.knology.net (24.42.128.1)  17.570 ms  10.788 ms  10.651
ms
 3  user-76-73-147-197.knology.net (76.73.147.197)  9.665 ms  10.274 ms  9.465 m
s
 4  user-24-96-198-18.knology.net (24.96.198.18)  9.819 ms  33.400 ms  34.325 ms
 5  user-24-96-110-161.knology.net (24.96.110.161)  17.161 ms  19.042 ms  14.486
ms
 6  user-75-76-127-174.knology.net (75.76.127.174)  16.362 ms  17.725 ms  13.858
ms
 7  dynamic-75-76-35-111.knology.net (75.76.35.111)  18.423 ms  25.521 ms  18.44
7 ms
 8  216.239.51.47 (216.239.51.47)  17.537 ms
    216.239.51.53 (216.239.51.53)  21.347 ms
    216.239.51.47 (216.239.51.47)  18.677 ms
 9  209.85.142.54 (209.85.142.54)  25.114 ms
    66.249.94.24 (66.249.94.24)  20.345 ms
    216.239.51.245 (216.239.51.245)  30.999 ms
10  209.85.248.53 (209.85.248.53)  18.709 ms
    209.85.142.65 (209.85.142.65)  23.750 ms
    216.239.56.164 (216.239.56.164)  19.681 ms
11  * * *
```

A. 74.125.21.113

B. 24.42.128.1

C. 192.168.1.1

D. 192.168.1.133

121. What would the server provide according to the following diagram?

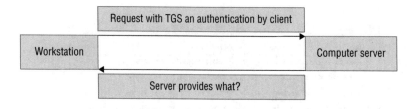

A. Server authentication

B. Key

C. Symmetric key

D. Access to client

122. As shown in the following image, who has both read and execute permissions for one object?

	OBJ 1	OBJ 2	OBJ 3	OBJ 4
SAVION	Read, write	write		execute
RAY J	execute		write	Read, write
SAMAREA	execute	execute	write	
RAELEAH	Read, write	read	Read,execute	

A. Raeleah

B. Samarea

C. Ray J

D. Savion

123. According to the following image, what browser is the user using?

A. Google Chrome

B. Internet Explorer

C. Mozilla Firefox

D. Opera

124. As shown in the following screen shot, which of these provides the alias record under the members.tripod.com zone?

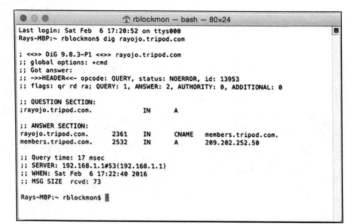

A. CNAME

B. A

C. rayojo.tripod.com

D. IN

125. In the following screen shot, what SSID is using the highest channel?

```
                                    🏠 rblockmon — bash — 119×23
Rays-MBP:~ rblockmon$ airport -s
                  SSID BSSID              RSSI CHANNEL HT CC SECURITY (auth/unicast/group)
           xfinitywifi 0c:54:a5:ee:f8:5a -86  6      Y US NONE
HP-Print-C2-Photosmart 6520 a0:d3:c1:c1:cb:c2 -87 10  Y -- WPA2(PSK/AES/AES)
              HOME-6512 cc:a4:62:d2:65:10 -70 11      Y US WPA(PSK/TKIP,AES/TKIP) WPA2(PSK/TKIP,AES/TKIP)
           xfinitywifi c6:a4:62:d2:65:10 -69 11      Y US NONE
              NETGEAR09 04:a1:51:ca:89:49 -88 10      Y -- WPA2(PSK/AES/AES)
              NETGEAR83 a0:63:91:ee:10:ba -80  8      Y -- WPA2(PSK/AES/AES)
           Linksys03034 48:f8:b3:e1:24:ef -80  7      Y -- WPA(PSK/AES,TKIP/TKIP) WPA2(PSK/AES,TKIP/TKIP)
      Linksys03034-guest 4a:f8:b3:e1:24:e0 -79  7      Y -- NONE
              HOME-3872 e8:ed:05:10:38:70 -85  6,+1   Y US WPA(PSK/TKIP,AES/TKIP) WPA2(PSK/TKIP,AES/TKIP)
           I can see you c4:04:15:1d:03:d4 -82  5      Y -- WPA2(PSK/AES/AES)
              Rokugan24 20:aa:4b:0e:bf:4f -37  6      N -- WPA(PSK/TKIP/TKIP)
              Rokugan24 84:1b:5e:39:0d:8f -52  6      N -- WPA(PSK/TKIP/TKIP)
               Kris-Com e0:46:9a:3f:54:f4 -75  4,+1   Y US WPA(PSK/AES,TKIP/TKIP) WPA2(PSK/AES,TKIP/TKIP)
           xfinitywifi 06:1d:d2:c4:15:70 -79  1      Y US NONE
              Allen202 e0:46:9a:34:ec:84 -86  1      Y -- WPA2(PSK/AES/AES)
              HOME-1572 00:1d:d2:c4:15:70 -79  1      Y US WPA(PSK/TKIP,AES/TKIP) WPA2(PSK/TKIP,AES/TKIP)
               Rokugan5 84:1b:5e:39:0d:90 -50 36      N -- WPA2(PSK/TKIP/TKIP)
Rays-MBP:~ rblockmon$
```

A. Rokugan5

B. Rokugan24

C. I can see you

D. Allen202

Appendix

Answers to Review Questions

Practice Test 1

1. **A.** Searching through the local paper is considered passive because it does not directly impact, alert, or establish any type of connection between the victim and the adversary.

2. **D.** The Rijndael cipher was selected and then named the Advanced Encryption Standard (AES).

3. **B.** Cain & Abel provides a suite of tools for password cracking and ARP poisoning, for example.

4. **D.** An IPS can have rules set that can dissect a packet to, for example, inspect the contents in hex or binary format.

5. **A.** Scanning the target network slowly prevents an IDS from alerting because the traffic may not be considered an anomaly. If the sensor sees a huge amount of traffic being generated, it may cause the sensor to alert; therefore, it is best practice to scan slowly.

6. **D.** Implementing an annual awareness training with the focus on social engineering will raise awareness in the organization. The training can be conducted by the information assurance section within the IT department.

7. **D.** The attacker would edit and/or delete log information during the covering tracks phase, which is the last phase during the attack.

8. **C.** The attacker is using the Nmap function to conduct a TCP connection scan on the target, which is part of the scanning and enumeration phase.

9. **C.** Unlike RC5 and RC6, RC4 is the stream block cipher—it is the only symmetric cipher that uses stream.

10. **A.** Receiving a formal written agreement is critical because it sets the legal limit of what is allowed and not allowed to be conducted. It protects the pentesters from legal action if they stay within the agreed work performance statement.

11. **C.** Elliptic Curve Cryptography requires less computational resources because it uses shorter keys compared with other asymmetric methods. It is often used in lower-power devices for this reason.

12. **B.** The SYN scan is used to detect open ports but does not complete the full three-way handshake. It is considered a "half open" connection.

13. **D.** The ARP request does not authenticate with the requested host; therefore, it is possible that the attacker can spoof the address of the victim with its own MAC address.

14. **D.** The most likely course of action is to restrict access to sensitive information. By doing so, you allow business services to continue while protecting user private data until a remediation can be performed.

15. **B.** If the attacker is successfully conducting a man-in-the-middle attack, he is currently maintaining access to the victim's network traffic.

16. A. Using SQL queries such ' or 1=1 is a method called fuzzing. This technique is used to test for SQL injection vulnerabilities.

17. B. The default TTL value for most Microsoft operating systems is 128.

18. D. Using the 1=1 value in the URL will test for SQL vulnerability that would allow the attacker to assume that the web application can implement arbitrary commands.

19. B. Using SSH is great for security, but in order to learn from what the adversary is doing is no longer feasible because of the encryption that is taking place.

20. D. The Ping of Death first appeared in 1996 because applications misinterpreted oversized packets.

21. A. The Melisa virus occurred on March 26, 1999, and quickly infected over 100,000 computers in a three-day span. The virus exploited the fact that macros were enabled by default within the Microsoft Office suite. Using the macro feature, the Melissa virus populated with ease when the victims opened their documents. The macro then executed and emailed contacts found within Microsoft Outlook, causing widespread infections.

22. A. If there is question whether a Windows PC has been compromised, a sure way to see what processes are being executed can be found within the Processes tab of Task Manager. Programs such as iexplore.exe are legitimate; however, some programs such as !explore.exe and explore.exe attempt to look legitimate to avoid detection.

23. D. In this scenario, you would choose the directional antenna because it focuses the radio transmission as a point-to-point link, unlike the omni antenna, which has 360-degree coverage. It also reduces the probability of an adversary conducting a war diving attack.

24. C. A checksum is a small size datum that is computed against the message itself and creates its own fingerprint. It is a means of detecting any changes in the message itself for integrity purposes. If the two checksums do not match, the message has been compromised. A checksum serves as a validation that no errors occurred.

25. A. RSA uses 1,024- and 2,048-bit key strengths as asymmetric encryption algorithms.

26. B. Digital Signature Authority (DSA) provides only nonrepudiation for emails. It does not provide confidentiality, integrity, or even authentication.

27. A. When a race condition occurs, either process may occur. If the timing is right, arbitrary commands may be executed with the current user level privileges until the next process begins.

28. B. If you are able to ping and even visit an external website using its IP address and not its fully qualified domain name (FQDN), it is more probable that the DNS sever is having issues. Check with the DNS server for functionality.

29. D. The administrator plugged in the intrusion prevention system (IPS) and applied too few rules. The administrator did not establish a baseline, which would have tailored the alerts to an appropriate level based on the LAN activity during certain hours of the day.

30. A. In a client-side attack, mobile code or some arbitrary command is sent from a server to a client for execution. Typically, you will see this carried out by the use of cross-site scripting (XSS). In this case, malicious code is transferred to a vulnerable web browser that is running on the client.

31. C. When black box testing is performed, only the penetration testing team and a few selected individuals know about it. The penetration test team does not know anything because this simulates a real-world threat against the company's network and incident response posture.

32. D. Although casing the target sounds right, the correct term for this activity is *reconnaissance*. In this phase, the attacker tries to gather all the facts they can about their target and answer any assumptions they may have through this activity.

33. A. Within the Ncat program, an adversary is able to conduct a sweeping array of scanning functions against a target system or range of hosts. It is more accurate than using Nmap or Netcat because Ncat can fingerprint the operating system and other special and unique features. Ncat is installed with most versions of the Linux distributions.

34. D. Using an open TCP connection scan, the attacker is trying to see what ports are open for connection. Because it is an open connection, the adversary does not attempt to resolve the three-way TCP connection. If the attacker chooses to do a full TCP connect, their address may be logged and can be traced.

35. B. Tapping a fiber line is very complicated. Unlike tapping into Ethernet, tapping into a fiber line could potentially drop network user traffic or even bring down the entire connection if too much light escapes the glass or plastic core.

36. B. Whenever you infiltrate a system, you would always want to cover your tracks by either editing or deleting your logs. This is important so the security administrators and investigators cannot trace your accounts, your location, and the methods you used to exploit the system.

37. A. If the adversary can capture the symmetric key used in Kerberos for an account, the adversary will have a wide arrange of access to network resources.

38. D. Passwords are located in the Security Account Manager (SAM) file, which is located in C:\Windows\system32\config. You may be able to retrieve the passwords from the C:\Windows\repair folder as well, even though this folder may not be available.

39. A. During an XMAS scan, the adversary would receive an RST response from the port if it is closed because the scan sends the FIN, URG, and the PSH flags.

40. D. By encoding the payload, the adversary is trying to avoid IDS/IPS detection because it changes the signature of the original payload to a different format.

41. D. The longer the password, the more it uses the advantage of the key space for encryption. Short complex passwords can be cracked within a reasonable amount of time. A password that is simple but longer will be exponentially harder to crack.

42. D. The adversary replaces the legitimate IP address for the domain name with the malicious IP address. The victim will not be aware of the switch because the domain name is being used and not the IP address.

43. C. With Cain & Abel, the adversary can forge certificates; however, the application lacks the ability to make the certificates look authentic. The user will be prompted, indicating that the certificate is not trusted.

44. D. The RC4 algorithm is used in WEP. Although RC4 is for the most part secure, the initialize vector is fairly short and therefore easily predictable. Cracking WEP will take a mere shared key.

45. B. The stranger is wardriving. Wardriving is the act of traveling with a high-powered antenna to pick up and use free or compromising weak Wi-Fi access points.

46. A. In a smurf attack, the adversary spoofs a victim's IP address. The adversary will then ping the broadcast address and all the nodes on the LAN respond back to the spoofed IP address of the victim. The result is a DoS attack on the victim's workstation.

47. D. When all the memory from the target server is drained, the server will not be able to process or store any information. This will eventually cause the server to freeze or crash, or it will possibly corrupt data. The end result is that none of the users will be able to use its resources.

48. A. If you look in the SAM file, after the username, the next value will be numerical. If it is a 500, this indicates that it is an administrator account.

49. D. The American Registry for Internet Numbers (ARIN) is one of the five domain name registrants and is responsible for North and South America.

50. A. After identifying live systems, detecting open ports, and detecting the operating systems and it services, you will then begin to scan for vulnerabilities.

51. C. An ICMP Type 8 code is an echo request that is used within the Ping application.

52. A. Ports 0 to 1023 are well known because they are what most services use. For example, port 80 is used for HTTP and port 53 for DNS.

53. B. The adversary dials telephone numbers to see what modems are opened. Modems can be a severe vulnerability to a network because they are either forgotten or used as a backup connection to systems.

54. A. The -s0 switch evokes Nmap to conduct an analysis of the target that is used to identify the operating system.

55. C. Using the command `net view /domain:<domain_name>` will retrieve all the systems that are joined to the domain.

56. B. The man is conducting a shoulder surfing attack. By looking over her shoulder, the man is able to pick up passwords and any other sensitive information that she is using on her tablet without her knowledge or approval.

57. A. The keyword UNION is a SQL command that joins two databases. In this case, you are joining the target database with your own malicious database. You might do something like this to steal credentials from the database for later use.

58. A. In a buffer overflow, data is written over its predetermined space in main memory. This could cause several different outcomes, including data corruption, system crashing, freezing, and other untold consequences.

59. A. A proxy server is a middleman between the private internal network and the untrusted network. By initiating the connection, it can provide core protections associated with web exploitations.

60. C. A honeypot is a server that is made to look like a legitimate target; however, it is configured to be vulnerable to an adversary's attack. The purpose is to learn about the adversary's methodologies of attack.

61. C. In Linux, the `lastlog` file is located in the `/var/log/` directory. This file contains the last user that was logged in, with all of their activity recorded.

62. A. The Secure Shell (SSH) application utilizes port 22 to establish a connection by default.

63. C. When you are conducting gray box testing, you have partial knowledge of the systems in play.

64. A. When conducting the firewalking technique, the user will adjust the TTL value passed 1 hop of the firewall. This will determine what ports are open on the firewall but will drop the packet when it hits the router.

65. D. Nmap is a tool that can be used to conduct scanning and other enumeration functions. It is capable of determining what ports and services are functional and, to a certain degree, what operating systems are installed on the host.

66. B. There are no port numbers associated with IP because it is a connectionless protocol.

67. C. Both IP and UDP are connectionless protocols. They do not form a connection-oriented bond between two ends.

68. A. A white hat is a pentester who works under a formal written agreement or a contract that legally sets the boundaries of what is to be tested and/or audited.

69. B. Patch management is actively testing patches in a testing environment and then deploying them into production. It also includes a fallback or rollback plan that is associated with patch management in case there were side effects that were not identified during the testing phase.

70. B. FTP occurs at the Application level along with Telnet and other application services.

71. A. The heart bleed attack leveraged a buffer overflow exploitation in order to push the service into replying with more payload data than designed. This results in data leakage.

72. A. Using the `-sX` switch causes Nmap to send packets with the FIN, PSH, and URG flags set.

73. C. Nmap uses a database of known characteristics that best matches the target to determine the operating system.

74. C. Cross-site scripting is an attack in which website visitors are infected through the web applications used on the target server. Most of the vulnerabilities are possible due to web browsers not being updated.

75. C. DNS, or Domain Name System, is an IP-to-name resolution service that utilizes port 53.

76. B. The passwd file stores general information about the user's account such as name and location.

77. D. In a packet analyzer such as Wireshark, the FIN flag can be viewed under the TCP section and then the Flags section.

78. D. The fraggle attack uses a spoofed source IP and UDP packets as its method of delivery because of speed and lack of error correction.

79. D. The 0x90 is an instruction that tells the CPU to move to the next set of instructions in main memory.

80. D. Using Telnet allows the adversary to enumerate services and versioning of a target system.

81. D. Broadcast is no longer used within IPv6 because of its inefficiency. IPv6 contains advanced protocols for host discovery.

82. B. A procedure is a step-by-step document that instructs the user to configure or set up a certain task or function.

83. D. FTP uses port 21 for commands and port 20 for data control.

84. A. Challenge-Handshake Authentication Protocol periodically challenges each other to determine authentication. It is used to prevent man-in-the-middle attacks.

85. A. User account provisioning is a life-cycle program in which users are reviewed and granted need-to-know and least-privilege access, and accounts are disabled or deleted. User accounts should be reviewed every 30 to 45 days to identify stale accounts.

86. D. An individual who is dumpster diving is looking through the trash container hoping to score important information. The adversary is counting on people throwing away vital information such as trade secrets without proper disposal handling. This act can become potentially difficult to manage because it can be completely legal to do so, depending on the circumstances.

87. B. Port 80 and 8080 are ports that are commonly used to connect to a web server. Although you can change this default port value, you face a very high risk of not having anyone connect unless it was designed that way for security purposes.

88. B. Although cloud computing is very versatile, it lacks the encompassing security posture one would think it may have. Because of the fact that you are depending on the commercial provider to enforce strict security practices and policies, you may actually never know what they are. One thing to keep in mind is that by using a free cloud solution, the contract that you agree to may very well provide cover for the provider from being sued by its customers for data loss, theft and damages, and other cyber incidents. Compared to a LAN solution, the administrators have proper oversight and management. Administrators can strictly enforce proper security measures, provide incident response at a moment's notice, and notify the population of events in a timely manner.

89.   D. An IP address combined with a port number is called a socket. Both are used to form a connection regardless of whether it's connection oriented or not.

90.   C. An object such as a file will have a classification level appended to it, depending on its value and sensitivity level. The classification level is used to allow access to someone who meets or exceeds the clearance level of the classification and has a "need to know" requirement. Using classification labels is a method of implementing access control when dealing with sensitive information.

91.   A. Cain & Abel allows the adversary or pentester to carefully craft their own certificates or have the application create its own, depending on the scenario. In either case, when prompted to accept the certificate from Cain & Abel, the browser will warn the user that this certificate has not been verified (trusted).

92.   D. RAID-2 uses hamming code, which does not provide any redundancy and requires using either 14 or 39 hard disks to implement. Because of the hard disk requirements, it is not fiscally acceptable due to other better and more capable RAID configurations available. Therefore, RAID-2 is primarily not used.

93.   C. Password Authentication Protocol (PAP) is a weak authentication protocol. It does not encrypt any data and the authentication credentials are sent in the clear. There is no method for challenging at either end; therefore, it is very easy to intercept and masquerade as a legitimate user.

94.   B. When implementing an identification process, "something you are" refers to biometric authentication. This is considered a Type 3 authentication factor.

95.   B. Whenever you are implementing more than one authentication factor, it is considered multifactor authentication. This means you are using two or more factors, such as "something you have," "something you know," and "something you are."

96.   A. MD5 is a hashing algorithm. It has no key associated with it, and therefore, it can be used by anyone. The purpose of hashing data is to provide a way to verify integrity, not origin.

97.   D. Security Onion is a Linux distribution based on Ubuntu. It uses an array of sensors and applications that can be customized to monitor and defend the network environment.

98.   A. Kali Linux (formerly known as BackTrack) is an operating system that is widely used by hackers and pentesters alike. It hosts a suite of tools aimed at scanning, target enumeration, and exploiting vulnerabilities.

99.   B. Antivirus software must be loaded with the latest virus definitions. Virus definitions are considered the DNA, or "signature," of known viruses. Without an updated virus signature in its database, the antivirus software does not know what new viruses are out in the wild.

100. D. Suricata is an IPS/IDS solution that you can use to defend your network. It comes pre-loaded with Security Onion and gives you the ability to operate an IPS/IDS appliance.

101. B. The total UDP packet size is 65,535. You must subtract 8 bytes from the UDP header and 8 bytes from the 28 byte IP header. The total UDP packet size is 65,535 bytes, so you subtract 28 bytes from the total size. This should give you a value of 65,507 for the total UDP payload size.

102. C. Using the classified section in the daily newspaper is an excellent way to footprint your target. Footprinting is the art of gathering facts about your intended target without illuminating yourself as the attacker or actively engaging your target.

103. B. When the target has an open port and receives a packet with the FIN flag set, the target will not respond with anything. That is because the target knows that the sender has finished communicating.

104. C. Most switches nowadays are able to defend against such an attack. For those that cannot, the switch's content addressable memory (CAM) will be flooded. This CAM table is where it learns the MAC address of hosts connected to its ports. When the switch is flooded with too many ARP requests, it will fail to open and operate as a hub. This will result in all of the information being broadcasted to all of the hosts connected to the switch. The adversary at this point can sniff LAN traffic.

105. D. The correct syntax to filter for a specific IP address is ip.addr ==.

106. D. Type 2 is a "something you have" access control method. This is associated with a token, common access card, or some other form of medium that you would you use to authenticate yourself.

107. B. An example of spear phishing is an email soliciting the user to click a link or reply back with sensitive information. Spear phishing targets individuals of high importance.

108. A. A botnet is a collection of zombie computers that are used in concert to conduct a distributed denial of service (DDoS) on a target system.

109. A. Physical controls are measures put in place to physically prevent someone from gaining access and entrance to a resource or a location.

110. D. The X.509 standard describes what and how certificates are created. It includes the version of the certificate, serial number, who issued it, and the type of signature algorithm used.

111. C. Steganography does not use encryption; however, it conceals or hides information within a picture or in an audio file.

112. A. In most cases, a honeypot will be classified as enticement because of the nature by which it is being employed. For this reason, administrators usually employ honeypots to lure in attackers and learn their hacking methodologies. The administrator will then create defensive measures in response to their newfound knowledge.

113. A. A wireless access point using an 802.11a standard will have an operating speed of 54 megabits per second (Mbps).

114. B. The body that issues the Certified Ethical Hacker certification is the EC-Council.

115. D. DHCP uses the UDP protocol because it is a connectionless service.

116. A. The Internet Assigned Numbers Authority (IANA) is the authority from which domains receive their identification. In this case, it is noted as the IANA Resgistrar ID 292.

117. D. The process identification (PID) number is located on the far left-hand column. In this case, Terminal has a PID of 1186.

118. B. In a distributed denial of service (DDoS) attack, the victim is bombarded with attacks from multiple bots.

119. D. The missing label in the middle arrow is the SYN/ACK, which is part of the three-way handshake. Without the SYN/ACK, a TCP connection cannot be established.

120. B. Under PID 0, the kernel_task is taking up 386 megabytes of memory from the system. This information is found under the MEM column.

121. A. The adversary who can successfully intercept and read traffic is conducting a man-in-the-middle attack. The purpose is to gain intelligence as long as possible without alerting the victim or IDS/IPS appliances.

122. B. The SYN stealth scanned 100 common ports, which is the most out of this particular Nmap scan.

123. A. The user's password file was hashed with SHA-512 and was salted. Using the salt function adds a pseudorandom value to the hashing algorithm that further secures and provides randomization to the output. This method adds another layer of security to prevent the hash from being brute-forced.

124. D. The owner has read and write privileges; group has read privileges; "others" have read privileges as well.

125. A. The TTL value is set at 64, which is normal for a Linux/Unix operating system. In the Ethernet frame, it shows the source as Apple_21:1d:0e, which now narrows our fingerprint to an OS X operating system.

Practice Test 2

1. C. An administrative control usually consists of policies or directives that give the organization a general format to comply with. For example, a security policy may state that the only means to log in to a workstation is through a common access card. An administrative control is also known as a soft control.

2. A. Using a /27, network administrators can successfully plan for 8 different networks. The octet value of a /27 is 32. If you count the bits in the Class C range (/25 is 128, /26 is 64, and /27 is 32), the total will be 224. Subtract 224 from 256 (the entire Class C octet value), which results in a value of 32. If you divide 256 by 32, you will receive 8, which is the number of subnets you can use, and 32 is the number of available addresses you can use per network.

3. B. Telnet uses a default port number of 23 for connection and communication.

4. A. When converting to binary, remember that we use only 0 to 9 and *A* to *E* in terms of hexadecimal value. Anything outside of that range is invalid.

5. A. Digital Signature Authority, or DSA, is an algorithm that is used to provide digital signatures on files and email to provide nonrepudiation and authenticity. It does not provide confidentiality or integrity.

6. C. The American Registry for Internet Numbers (ARIN) is the organization that tracks and records all matters that deal with Internet matters for North America and surrounding territories. It tracks IPv4, IPv6, and autonomous system numbers as well.

7. D. Address Resolution Protocol, or ARP, is utilized at the Network layer because querying computers for their IP address is directly related to the Network layer in the OSI model.

8. B. A fence standing 8 feet tall with razor wire is considered a preventative measure because the goal is to prevent the adversary from entering the premises. It is not considered a deterrent because deterrents do not keep a persistent adversary out.

9. D. The IEEE 802.11i standard does not define a Wi-Fi spectrum; it amends to the 802.11 standard to include and implement Wi-Fi Protected Access II (also known as WPA2).

10. A. Read is set to 4, write is set to 2, execute is set to 1, no permission is set to 0. The value for Read and execute would be 4 and 1 which equals 5.

11. A. DHCP follows this simple process: the client *discovers* a DHCP server, the DHCP server *offers* an IP address to the client, the client *requests* that IP address for usage, and the server *acknowledges* the leasing of the offered IP address to the client. The IP address is then removed from the DHCP leasing pool and is no longer reserved.

12. B. The AES algorithm uses 128-, 192-, and 256-bit key space for encryption.

13. C. A logic bomb is malware that lies dormant until a certain event is cued, such as date, time, keystrokes, or even opening applications in a sequential order.

14. A. The majority of botnets are managed by the Internet Relay Chat (IRC) application, which functions as a chat room. Using this capability, the bot or zombie master is able to send commands and control functions to their bots.

15. B. This policy is called the clean desk policy. It is widely used in industries where it's important to keep confidential and sensitive information secured by cleaning up before the work day ends. It prevents coworkers, cleaning crews, and other bystanders from pilfering and mishandling critical information.

16. D. An intranet provides access to the organization's internal network and network applications.

17. A. A circuit-level gateway operates at the Session layer because that is the OSI layer that sets up, establishes, and terminates sessions.

18. C. With an incremental backup, only files with the archived bit set are backed up. Only the files that have been changed since the last backup are chosen to be archived.

19. C. *Impersonation* is term that is associated with masquerading. It is not considered identity theft because it doesn't involve personally identifiable information (PII) such as Social Security numbers and birthdates. The attacker merely uses a means of communication such as a phone call to fool the victim into believing that they are who they say they are.

20. B. A rootkit is malware that embeds itself at the kernel level. It is extremely difficult to discover and remediate because of the inherent security measures that are present at the beginning in the kernel.

21. D. The Trusted Platform Module (TPM) is a chip that is soldered onto the motherboard with preprogrammed cryptographic keys. It allows the hard drive that is bonded to the motherboard to be accessible. If the hard drive is removed, it will not be accessible by any other means.

22. A. A dictionary attack is the fastest method because the adversary has a file loaded with the most commonly used passwords. Because this file is finite in nature, this type of attack does not always work. For a guaranteed way of cracking an account, the adversary may resort to the brute force method, but this can take much longer than other methods, and in most cases, it's not even feasible.

23. C. The user identifier, or UID, is the designator that uniquely identifies each user on the workstation.

24. D. Using Nmap, the -sU switch command allows for the administrator to scan for UDP connections on a target workstation. If you receive an ICMP message of "port unreachable," it means that the port is closed.

25. B. A top-level parent is usually represented as .org, .com, .net, .gov, and .edu. Countries also have their own parent domains, such as .ru for Russia and .kr for South Korea.

26. C. When Telnet is being used, traffic is sent in the clear, which is not beneficial because information can be compromised. This is, however, beneficial to the security administrator because they can see exactly what methods and activities the adversary is using in Telnet. When SSH came on board, it removed the capability of eavesdropping on the connections the adversary was using ,and thus the security administrator lost situational awareness because the traffic was encrypted.

27. D. All though a DoS or DDoS is the actual result of the attack, the reason is that the adversary is conducting a SYN flood attack.

28. A. "Network Unknown" falls under the ICMP Type 3 (Destination Unreachable), Code 6 category.

29. B. Frequency-hopping spread spectrum is a process in which the receiver frequently hops around the frequency spectrum to avoid jamming, creating interference, and eavesdropping. The client needs to be on the same timing source as the broadcaster or the client will not be able to match the intervals in which the frequency changes.

30. C. The chances of the adversary conducting similar probing techniques on your servers from different locations is an indication that the adversary is using a web proxy service. The adversary is trying to mask their actual IP address in order to escape possible prosecution and other legal actions.

31. C. Whois.net is a free service that you can use to capture critical information for part of your footprinting when targeting a victim.

32. A. RFC 18 covers non-routable IP addresses which are the private IP addresses. Private IP addresses are 10.0.0.0–10.255.255.255, 172.16.0.0–172.31.255.255, and 192.168.0.0–192.168.255.255.

33. A. Type 8 is the formal ICMP echo request. There is no code associated with it. Type 8 Code 0 =, which is the ICMP echo reply.

34. A. In most cases, a host-based intrusion detection system (HIDS) uses a signature base detection method to protect the host. Most HIDS, such as Tripwire and CyberSafe, download the newest rules to the client to provide protection; however, the HIDS falls sort when defending against zero day attacks because of no known countermeasure as of yet.

35. D. In a PKI environment, the registration authority (RA) is the subject that validates a user and then vouches for their authenticity to the certificate authority, which then releases a certificate.

36. D. The method of cracking or breaking an encryption algorithm to discover either the key and/or the backdoor is called cryptanalysis.

37. D. Whenever we XOR a bit, if the two inputs are the same such as 1 and 1 or 0 and 0, then the XOR return value, or output, will always equal 0. If the two input values are different, such as 1 and 0 or 0 and 1, the return value will always be 1.

38. B. In promiscuous mode, the network adapter does not alter any of the frames that it receives. It simply just copies the frames for analysis using a protocol analyzer such as Wireshark.

39. A. The Cipher Block Chaining Message Authentication Code Protocol is an algorithm that uses a 128-bit key, which is based on the AES algorithm.

40. D. In a fraggle attack. the adversary forges the source address, which is the web server. The adversary will then ping the broadcast address, which causes all of the clients in that subnet to respond back to the web server. This in turn causes a DDoS, but it is not the culprit. The actual attack was caused by the adversary through packet crafting and forging the source IP address of the web server.

41. A. The final event in establishing the TCP three-way handshake is ACK.

42. A. A token is a Type 1 authentication factor, which is "something you have."

43. B. Pharming is an attack in which you direct users to a website that looks legitimate. The goal is to trick the users into entering their credentials so that you can use them at a later date. One tool that is designed to do this is Metasploit's Social Engineering framework.

44. A. If you reuse a protocol analyzer and craft a packet for an XMAS scan using URG, PSH, and FIN, you will see in the TCP header the binary format of 00101001 being set.

45. A. Soft controls usually consist of policies, procedures, guidelines, or regulations that put in or recommend control measures for effective governance.

46. D. When a backdoor is installed, it allows the adversary to conduct remote call procedures such as a reverse terminal session or remote desktop procedures. The adversary can then conduct arbitrary operations as if they are logged in locally.

47. C. Biometrics is the method of collecting and using human characteristics such as fingerprints, facial recognition, and speech pattern in order to provide authentication for system access.

48. C. RC4 is a stream symmetric cryptography stream. It is the only stream cipher in the symmetric category. RC5 and RC6 are block cipher encryption algorithms.

49. A. Digital Signature Authority, or DSA, uses symmetric encryption to provide nonrepudiation. The recipient would use their key to decrypt the hash. Then the recipient would hash the value and compare it to the sender's hash. If the hash values match, the recipient knows that the message is authentic and came from the sender.

50. B. The inherent flaw in WEP is the IV, because it is only 24 bits long and transmitted in clear text. Using a tool call Aircrack, you can successfully exploit the vulnerability in WEP's poor IV design; you can crack WEP within 2 minutes.

51. D. Enumeration is the act of actively engaging the target system and gathering information.

52. A. Using nmap, the switch -sP is a ping sweep command and -O is the command to fingerprint the operating system.

53. C. POP3 is reserved for port 110. POP3 is a client/server protocol used to push email to clients.

54. D. Dig is the command used to query information about a server using its domain name.

55. B. For DNS queries, geektools.com is a sufficient resource to gain intelligence about your intended target. Whois (www.whois.net) is another popular site for DNS queries.

56. A. Telnet is an application you can use to conduct banner grabbing. If Telnet is operational on the target system, even though port 23 may be closed, it is possible to learn what type of server is being used to host by using port 80 if you are probing a web server.

57. C. Giving the owner a list of vulnerabilities is the correct answer because patched systems, disabled accounts, and revoked certificates are objects that are already accounted for.

58. C. IEEE 802.1x is the protocol for port-base network access that requires authentication.

59. B. Bonk uses UDP crafted packets to conduct a DoS on a Windows system. The UDP packets are oversized and when reconstructed can cause a crash on the target server.

60. A. A worm is an application that does not need a host or other resources from the computer to carry out its payload. It is a self-contained application, and it only needs to be introduced to the computer once to exploit the vulnerabilities found.

61. B. Adware is an application that continuously generates advertisement windows as pop-ups on the client. Most anti-spyware and antivirus products provide remedies to these threats.

62. D. Security posture is the level at which an organization can withstand a cyberattack. Some have a very low security posture, meaning that if they were to come under attack, most likely it will be detrimental. If an organization has a very high security posture, they are more capable of defending and warding off the adversary.

63. A. An SSO strategy could allow an adversary to conduct a DoS against the SSO service, making authentication and domain access difficult if not impossible until remediation occurs, which impacts many interdependent applications.

64. D. Type 4 is known as "somewhere you are" and is a method of validation using GPS.

65. B. By following the TCP stream using a protocol analyzer such as Wireshark, you are able to filter out the packets by determining when a new TCP session occurs.

66. C. A content-addressable memory table, or CAM table, is a table that contains a list of MAC addresses that are registered to a point on a layer 2 switching device.

67. A. In a ping of death attack, the adversary sends fragments of an ICMP message that when put together, create an oversized message. When the victim recompiles the message, the system crashes because it does not know how to process an ICMP message that is oversized.

68. C. Kerberos is an AAA server that uses symmetric keys. If the adversary is able to compromise the Kerberos server, it is possible that they can replay stolen credentials.

69. A. Network address translation (NAT) is a protocol that is used to change a private IP address to a public IP address when it leaves the LAN for Internet services. Since there is usually one public IP address that can be used to service multiple private IP clients, the clients are given a random port number that is 1024 or greater if they are waiting for a response from the Internet.

70. D. Host IDS and network IDS are the only two types of IDSs. They are used to alert administrators about possible intrusions. They do not, however, prevent them.

71. A. First you must calculate the single loss expectancy (SLE), which is $10,000,000 (asset value) divided by 50% (exposure factor), which equals $5,000,000. Then you multiply your SLE ($5,000,000) by 10% (annual rate of occurrence), which gives you an ALE of $500,000.

72. B. Health Insurance Portability and Accountability Act (HIPAA) is a federal regulation that mandates that all medical PII must be secured using encryption and other controls during transit and at rest. Failure to comply with the regulation can mean drastic consequences, such as jail time and heavy fines being imposed.

73. A. Time is one advantage the adversary will always have. They are on the offensive, and the more time they take to understand and develop their method of attack against the system, the more they increase their probability of success.

74. B. IEEE 802.1x is most associated with client authentication in wireless networks; however, it can also be used in an 802.3 environment.

75. D. Using DROP in the SQL query causes the database to completely erase the corresponding table. In this case, the adversary who uses DROP TABLE Clients tells the SQL database to delete the table called Clients.

76. C. Nessus is an application that is used to conduct vulnerability scans against a target host or a range of hosts on a subnet.

77. C. A Yagi antenna is the same as a directional antenna. You would choose a directional antenna over the Omni directional because of two reasons: One, you gain further power and throughput; two, the signal is propagated in only one direction and not in a 360-degree fashion where anybody in range can pick it up. With a directional antenna, the adversary would have to be in line of sight to pick up the traffic.

78. B. Phil Zimmerman created the Pretty Good Privacy (PGP) algorithm. At one point in time he was subjected to legal action by the United States government for not handing over the algorithm. Instead, Zimmerman published the algorithm on the Internet for anyone to use for free.

79. D. IPv6 has an address scheme of 128 bits. Due to its size, it can provide an IP address to every single person on Earth, with even more to spare. It also eliminated the broadcast protocol and implemented native features such as IP security.

80. B. A system that has a vulnerability means that there is no countermeasure or safeguard in place. If there is a safeguard or countermeasure in place, then there is no vulnerability present.

81. A. Whenever a user climbs higher in an organization and retains and gains more privileges without being subjected to a need-to-know and least-privilege rule, it's called scope creep. Administrators must constantly audit user access in their organization to defend against possible incidents.

82. A. *Node* is a general term for indicating a device that is connected to a network. It can be a computer, a router, a switch, a hub, or even a printer.

83. B. Spyware is malware that is used to collect critical information about a user, such as credit card numbers, user credentials, and even personally identifiable information.

84. A. The SSID can hold 32 characters. It has no form of authentication, but it is case sensitive for association purposes so a client can be joined to the access point.

85. D. IKE is a protocol in IPsec that allows for two clients to exchange secret keys to establish a VPN connection.

86. A. The crossover error rate (CER) is the point at which the FRR and the FAR intersect. This means that the settings for the biometric device are set at an optimal setting for authenticating subjects.

87. D. A Trojan is malware that is disguised to look like a legitimate application that is installed on a system. Oftentimes it can be overlooked, but an antivirus or anti-malware scanner with an up-to-date definition can pick up on the malware unless it is a zero day malware package.

88. C. Secure FTP uses TCP port 22, which is also utilized by Secure Shell (SSH). This is the preferred method of file transit if security is a concern.

89. A. IEEE 802.3 uses the Carrier Sense Multiple Access with Collision Detection (CSMA/CD) method to reduce traffic and implement packet recovery. It is also used in Ethernet networks.

90. B. A logic bomb was initiated because of a sequence of events that caused the system to become inoperable, forcing the users to manually shut down their system.

91. A. LDAP, which is the Lightweight Directory Access Protocol, uses port 389. Microsoft Active Directory-Directory Service uses LDAP in this manner.

92. B. The certificate authority is the system responsible for creating certificates and signing them on behalf of the subject requesting it.

93. A. Need to know is a policy/methodology that gives access to information to only certain individuals who need the information to perform their duties.

94. D. Macros should be disabled because they can be used to execute arbitrary code that can be malicious, such as a macro virus.

95. C. An escrow is a third-party entity that is trusted to hold and secure keys in case there is concern that the primary site will be destroyed or a possibility that the vendor will go out of business. You would typically use a key escrow as a backup solution for keeping keys secure.

96. A. HTTPS uses the standard port 443 for browsing the Internet with certificate PKI encryption.

97. D. Single sign-on (SSO) is a method used to allow users to authenticate once and have access to multiple resources. If it's not used, the user would have to continuously enter their credentials to get access to resources, which can be cumbersome.

98. B. A router is used to separate broadcast domains. This allows a single router to have multiple networks and keep network traffic at a minimum.

99. C. ICMP does not use ports.

100. C. The CPU cache is the most volatile out of the group. Memory such as DDR3 and other slot modules on the motherboard can retain data residue, but only for a very short while, and then it is zeroed out.

101. D. The SAM file is the object that contains the list of passwords for users who reside on the current system. It contains the user account information along with their Security Identification (SID).

102. A. Brute forcing is a method used to try every single combination of letters, numbers, and special characters to determine the password. It is the only method that will absolutely work.

103. B. The sum of the binaries for read, write, and execute is 7. The owner, group, and others would each receive a numeral 7 to indicate read, write, and execute privileges on a target object.

104. C. The GRUB is the application that executes at startup and prompts the user to choose which operating system to boot with.

105. A. Metasploit is considered a framework for pen testing. There are many different ways to accomplish a certain task that a pentester or an adversary may use against a target system or a network.

106. D. Using the attribute command attrib plus the switch that signifies to hide, +h, you would type the name of the file you want to hide. It is then only accessible to the owner of the file at that point. Another option is to open the file's properties and toggle the Hidden check box as well.

107. A. The MAC address has six allocations for the address and a range from 0 to 9 and *A* to *F*.

108. D. A packet layer firewall operates at the Network layer of the OSI model. It determines who is permitted or denied entry or exit based upon the IP address.

109. A. A honeynet is a network that is designed to look like a legitimate network with security misconfigurations made. It is designed to entice and allow the adversary to explore the network and covertly capture their methods and trade-craft used and further enhance their security posture.

110. B. Anti-malware software is a great tool; however, if a system is infected with a zero day exploit or virus, the anti-malware will not be able to defend against it because it does not recognize the malware signature.

111. A. Data encryption algorithm (DEA) is the actual name of the algorithm. The encryption used, though, is the Data encryption standard.

112. A. Heart Bleed is a reverse buffer overflow in which the target server is exploited by having its memory contents delivered to the adversary. This exploit can be used to discover passwords and other critical information that should not be delivered to the adversary.

113. B. Ransomware is a type of malware that encrypts the target system. It then asks the victim to send money to receive the key to unlock their system.

114. D. IEEE 802.11n uses both 2.4 and 5 GHz frequency and produces a rated speed of 100 Mbps.

115. A. Public key infrastructure (PKI) uses certificate authorities (CAs) and registration authorities (RAs) to validate, sign, and issue certificates to users in their domain.

116. B. Under the Ethernet (layer 2 header), the sender is broadcasting an ARP request.

117. B. Under the EN1, the IP address is given as 192.168.1.118 and it has a broadcast address of 192.168.1.255.

118. D. When you are observing the file source on a web page, the meta charset will show what encoding type is being used. In this case, it is using the UTF-8 encode method.

119. A. In the SSL header, the TLS version is determined to be 1.2 after the security association was reestablished.

120. C. Entering certain characters such as an ' or 1=1 can provide clues about whether a website is vulnerable to SQL injection. In this case, we received an error from the SQL database, which means it is vulnerable to SQL injection.

121. B. The adversary in this case in trying to redirect their position from the web server to the actual file system itself. Using the cmd.exe application, they are trying to gain access to the Windows terminal for arbitrary command execution.

122. A. In the Domain Name System section, you can determine that www.google.com is being used as a DNS resolution for this scenario.

123. C. The /etc/passwd file does not show the passwords for the accounts on the system. Passwords are stored in the /etc/shadow file in hash format.

124. A. The traffic of the data is annotated by the ->, which is the direction in which the file is being downloaded. The socket address is 172.16.1.100:49190.

125. B. The user ray is a valid user account. You can determine the user in in the /etc/shadow if there is hash value associated with the subject's account. In this case, our hash begins with 6xHEKhMr2.

Practice Test 3

1. D. The Simple Network Management Protocol is a protocol that is used with network appliances and nodes. You can gather statistical, performance, and status updates from your devices with this protocol.

2. B. An extranet is a subnet that functions like a DMZ, but it allows two businesses that depend on one another to share resources.

3. D. A Class C subnet has 256 bits. Subtracting 192 bits from 256 bits results in 64 hosts per subnet. Dividing 256 by 64 provides 4 usable networks.

4. B. The file location is /etc/shadow, and it contains a list of passwords that are hashed. In most cases, this file is hidden if you are not in the root account.

5. D. When you enter the command su root, you are prompted with the root password. If it's entered correctly, you can switch from your profile to the root account and have administrator-level privileges on the operating system.

6. B. TLS uses RSA 1024 or the 2048-bit key strength. In most web browsers, you are able to view this information in the Security tab in the preferences panel.

7. A. A baseline must be set in order for an anomaly detection system to run optimally. If not, the IDS will not be able to monitor network traffic accurately and may alert due to false positives.

8. D. The MX, or Mail Exchange, is the record that is used in a DNS server to identify the actual mail server.

9. C. The CPU cache contains the least amount of memory, and it is only used for instructions that are mostly used by the CPU. Most CPU caches hold anywhere from 512 KB of memory to 2 MB or more.

10. A. Not utilizing employee rotation and enforcing mandatory vacations can cause significant threat issues such as fraud, waste, and abuse.

11. A. The zero-day was successful due to the web server being compromised. The first order of action would be to remediate any vulnerabilities and ensure that these systems are no longer infected or compromised.

12. A. HKEY_LOCAL_MACHINE\SAM is the Registry entry where the SAM and SAM.log parameters can be found.

13. C. When scanning for SNMP using Metasploit, the command is use `auxiliary/ scanner/snmp/<device name>`. Once that is set, you will set your listening and receiving host information and then execute the scan by entering run into the command line.

14. B. In the command line, when searching for a particular string, you use the `grep` command to search for contents. Most often, administrators would pipe the string into another command or to an output format such as a text document.

15. D. When you're using `msfencode` in Metasploit, the payload will be converted into a raw output format. Encoding the payload allows the signature of your malware to be changed, greatly increasing your ability to be detected by signature-based technologies.

16. A. A reverse shellcode, or a "callback" shellcode, is an exploit that is used to have the victim initiate the connection with the adversary. This is a feasible way of establishing a connection because internal-to-external connections are usually not blocked by the firewall.

17. B. Buffers provide data storage capacity. When data is allocated to that storage and is found to be too large, it causes a buffer overflow in which arbitrary commands can be executed or data can be overwritten.

18. A. `Strcpy` is a function that is used in C that allows a variable or an input value that will be assigned to a constant. In this case, `exploit_this` is being assigned to the `attacker` variable.

19. B. Boundary checking is validating all input. If a user inputs a value that is greater than the memory allocated for it, the program will return with an invalid operation. It will continue to do so until the user inputs a value that is within the specified container value.

20. C. It is highly recommended to initialize variables with a value that is constant, such as 0 (zero), or another value that is pertinent to its function. If you don't initialize the variable, data residue may still be present and when it comes time to execute a set of instructions, the data output may not be accurate.

21. D. Heaps are used during the execution of a program. Because a program can have dynamic processes, heaps are used to allocate the amount of memory for it.

22. B. Programs that are initially executed have a segment in memory allocated called a stack. A stack has a fixed allocation of memory when it is created.

23. A. In order for the adversary to get passed segment violations, they would have to use NOP sleds to move the pointer past a point where their instructions can be executed.

24. C. Whenever the adversary is trying to knock a system offline by any means, it is generally called a denial of service; however, the method that they use can vary in many different ways.

25. A. Session hijacking is associated with TCP/IP because of the three-way handshake. Because of this, if the adversary is able to correctly guess the session value, it is very possible to interject themselves in between and then take over as one of the users. UDP does not have a three-way handshake, and IP is a connectionless protocol by itself.

26. A. The adversary must first track the session before making a successful attempt at hijacking it.

27. A. ISO 27002 (formerly 17799) is the standard that lays out guidelines for information system security managers who initiate, put into action, and maintain information security within an organization.

28. C. Key loggers come in hardware and software packages. They are used to covertly capture the victim's key strokes at a terminal to be later retrieved by the adversary to replay their credentials.

29. C. Community strings contain data that provides authentication. Depending on the type of string, it will provide the user with a certain level of privileges. For example, the public community string derives only a read-only privilege.

30. C. A Canonical Name (CNAME) record provides an alias to a domain name.

31. A. Adware is a type of malware that creates pop-up windows on the desktop to advertise for commercial products.

32. B. Availability ensures that data is readily available to the customer.

33. D. A proxy server is a device that acts a buffer between an untrusted and a trusted network. All connections are initiated from either side and handed off to the proxy server to establish and maintain.

34. A. XPTools is an application that provides steganography in order to secure a message through a picture, file, or some other format.

35. A. LOIC, or Low Orbit Ion Cannon, is an application that can be used to conduct a DDoS on a system by using TCP, UDP, or HTTP requests.

36. D. The UPDATE command is used to update data in a record in a table. Depending on the situation, the adversary can add, create, or even change an administrator's password in a SQL database.

37. C. The Others group allows a user to assign those who do not fall in the Group category access to an object.

38. B. John the Ripper is a program that allows an individual to crack an account. It is lightweight and can be found on Kali Linux.

39. B. The Internet segment is the third layer in the TCP/IP model which is equivalent to the Network layer in the OSI model.

40. B. The FIN flag set informs the distant end to terminate its connection with the sender. No action will be taken after it is set.

41. A. Angry IP is an application that provides an array of tools for ping sweeping. Depending on the configuration, there is a good chance an IPS/IDS appliance illuminating your presence conducting ping sweeps will be detected.

42. A. Cain & Abel is an application that provides an array of tools to the user, such as tools for password cracking, ARP spoofing, and conducting man-in-the-middle attacks.

43. B. Red teams traditionally provide the penetration testing function for a customer or an organization.

44. B. Identity theft is the process in which the adversary impersonates the victim in order to gain some type of access to the victim's financial resources or other critical resources.

45. A. BackTrack used to be the primary distribution for a hacker or pentester to use. Since then, it has been replaced with Kali Linux. Security Onion is most associated with defender or detection toolkits.

46. C. The first step is conducting a passive recon on your target system in order to build out the footprint.

47. B. NIST, or National Institute of Standards and Technology, is a government organization that provides standards to an array of industries, including standards for information systems management and cryptology.

48. A. Tiger team consists of representatives from the organization who are tasked to identify and resolve key issues in the organization. They can also be referred to as a task force.

49. D. Covert channels are used to send data in a manner that does not follow security practices and policies. In this case, the user or process is evading protective measures in order to ensure that their malicious activity is successful.

50. D. An ECHO reply is the response back from when a user sends a ping command to a node.

51. C. When clients communicate directly with one another without the aid of a wireless access point, they are communicating in ad hoc mode.

52. D. Promiscuous mode allows the wireless adapter to receive the packets, read them, and then forward them to the WAP. The wireless adapter in this case does not alter any of its information.

53. A. Manipulation is the process of tricking the victim to conduct a certain action that is favorable in compromising their account or system.

54. D. Vulnerability means that something lacks a defensive mechanism or a countermeasure.

55. C. An ATM card is part of a Type 1 authentication factor because it's something you have, and a Type 2 because it can only be used with your knowledge of the PIN.

56. B. When an account may have been compromised, it is recommended to disable and change the password in order to prevent the reuse of credentials.

57. D. Firewalls are configured out of the box with an implicit deny all policy. The security administrator will configure the rules to have the firewall implement after the fact.

58. B. SID2User is an application that can query the SID that is located in the SAM file if the username is provided. It was developed by Evgenii Rudny.

59. A. Port 53 is used to conduct DNS resolutions and zone transfers.

60. A. An adversary who continuously dials random numbers to connect to a modem is trying to gain unauthorized access. Modems are often forgotten about and therefore are more than likely not secured.

61. C. UDP does not use the RST flag that is reserved for the TCP protocol.

62. D. Traceroute is a useful tool because it will tell the administrator what path the packets are taking and possibly inform the administrator of firewalls within its path.

63. A. TTL is a protocol that prevents packets from flooding the Internet. A value such as 64 is assigned, and every time the packet reaches a router, the value decrements by 1. When it reaches zero, the router will drop the packet.

64. B. NS delegates DNS zones that work with authoritative name servers.

65. B. The -sI switch allows the user to conduct an idle scan. It is used to gather the IP address of the target system by crafting special packets that are bounced off a zombie machine.

66. C. Gap analysis compares the potential performance to an actual performance. This allows management to decide whether or not to allocate more resources, pull back, or look again at the entire planning and implementation process.

67. D. Hot sites provide an organization with all the necessary equipment to be used in the event of a disaster. It is a turnkey solution that requires only the personnel to resume company operations.

68. D. Broadcast domains are separated by using routers, and that most likely entails using its own interfaces and its corresponding network segment as well.

69. C. A private key is known to one person and only one person. It is used in the asymmetric encryption algorithms.

70. A. The Trusted Platform Module (TPM) is specially designed hardware that binds by using encryption. If another hard drive is swapped, the motherboard will not allow the hard drive to boot. And if the hard drive is connected to another motherboard, the motherboard will not recognize it and will fail to boot.

71. D. SMAC is a tool that will allow the ability to temporarily spoof the MAC address on a network interface card.

72. A. Direction antennas are also known as Yagi antennas, and they are used to provide an ad hoc solution to bridge wireless networks.

73. B. SNMPv3 is the latest installment for network appliance management. It adapts encryption and user authentication in order to make configurations and polling operations.

74. D. An evil twin is a wireless access point that is made to look like an actual legitimate WAP. The adversary is tempting users to reconnect to it by having the victims send their credentials. The adversary hopes to gain financial information when the victims conduct e-commerce transactions.

75. A. The Iran nuclear centrifuges were infected with the Stuxnet viruses. It caused the centrifuges to spin out of control, causing irrecoverable physical damage.

76. A. Wrappers allow malware to be concealed in legitimate programs that would most likely be opened without caution from the user and often remain to function as intended.

77. D. Physical controls are used to restrict, prevent, or deny access. In this case, lights, bollards, and fences are an external physical control.

78. B. POODLE, which stands for Padding Oracle on Downgraded Legacy Encryption, exploits the SSL 3.0 requests. After the last request, the attacker will be able to retrieve 1 byte of data that is between the client and server.

79. B. Tor is a network comprising volunteered private routers that build a network based on confidentially and is free to use. Tor was developed in the mid-1990s by the United States Naval Research Laboratory.

80. C. A ticket-granting service provides access to a subject for a certain resource or object.

81. A. A signature-base IDS must have an up-to-date signature list to accurately alert and defend against attacks.

82. C. A backoff timer is used to allow other nodes to complete their transmission. The backoff timer is a pseudorandom value that counts down and then tries to transmit again.

83. D. Bodo Moller, Thai Duong, and Krysztof Kotowicz published the vulnerability to the public domain on October 14, 2014.

84. B. Heartbleed was issued as CVE-2014-0160 and was reported on April 1, 2014.

85. C. An executive summary is a high-level view of the overall penetration testing results. It is geared toward senior officials and managers.

86. D. Separation of duties is the principle that requires two or more people to perform a task. These tasks are usually tied to a sensitive action such as making a large deposit in a bank or even launching nuclear weapons from a submarine. It prevents one person or entity from having complete unadulterated control over a task or function.

87. B. Remediation is the level of security posture where you correct systems that have been compromised by either malware, system malfunction, or some other unwanted incident.

88. C. Category I's (Roman numeral) are vulnerabilities that will lead to a root-level system access. This type of vulnerability category should be remediated right away in order to prevent the adversary from escalating and conducting more sophisticated attacks on your system and even your network.

89. D. Availability is part of the triad that deals with how easy or difficult it is to use resources or data. The easier it is to access data, the less secure it may be, but it's also true that the harder it is to access, the less likely it will be compromised and the more likely work production will be slowed down.

90. C. Even though using a shredder is a physical control to prevent information from being leaked, a mandatory policy was used to get the organization to confirm.

91. B. Port Address Translation (PAT) uses the source computer's port address as a unique web session when the packet leaves the local network.

92. A. The macro feature that was once enabled by default when you installed Microsoft Office is now disabled. The I Love You virus took advantage of that capability by capturing contacts in users' email address books and sending out mass copies of itself to those recipients.

93. C. Type 4, or "somewhere you are," is part of the process of authenticating a user or subject. It does not necessarily involve using a GPS tracking system to validate a subject. A subject can also be validated by using cellular towers to triangulate their position.

94. B. In Linux, the / set by itself denotes that the user is currently residing in the root directory.

95. A. Role-based access control, or RBAC, is an access control model that is developed around a job position. For example, if you worked at a bank as a teller, your login resources are tailored to what a bank teller would have access to. It is a cookie-cutter type of profile that aids in controlling employee access and limits capabilities to do one and only one job.

96. D. Passive reconnaissance is the act of gathering as much knowledge and intelligence you can without directly impacting operations of the target. Although it is much harder to gather information through this phase, it almost guarantees that as a black hat, you and your operation will not be compromised.

97. C. The rule head defines the rule type, protocol, source IP and port, the direction, and then the destination IP address and the port.

98. A. Time to live (TTL) is a value set on IP packets that decrements each and every time they pass through a router. Some operating systems, such as Linux and Microsoft, will set the TTL value. When the TTL value of a packet reaches 0, that packet will be dropped and an ICMP "Destination Not Found" message will be returned to the source.

99. B. When the security administrators are no longer following the security policies set in place by the organization, it is a telltale sign that the policies are not up to date. Policies should be evaluated often because the operational tempo and working environment can be and will be dynamic.

100. C. Session, or fragmentation, splicing is the process of breaking up a payload among different packets that the IDS may ignore. When the host receives all of the packets and processes them, the exploit may trigger the arbitrary payload the adversary has sent, such as installing malware or providing a reverse command shell.

101. A. If a switch receives too many sets of instructions and it cannot keep up with the demand, it fails open. Fail open is when the switch does not separate traffic anymore by collision domains and thus will flood out all the traffic to all of the ports, much like a hub. If the adversary can do this, they can now receive all the traffic that is broadcasted from all of the computers connected to the switch.

102. D. The -sS conducts a port scan, and the -O scans the system and fingerprints for an operating system type.

103. B. ToneLoc is one of the popular applications that allows an adversary to search and conduct war dialing operations for potential modem connections that were once forgotten about.

104. C. Probing the firewall with ACK flagged messages will determine what the firewall blocking is for. More often than not, Linux operating systems use the ACK method that determines if the destination is unreachable by using the ICMP protocol.

105. C. Qualitative risk analysis evaluates risks that are tied to your intangible assets. For example, not setting up an encryption program for your organization to use threatens the security of your customers' PII and can tarnish your company's reputation.

106. A. IEEE 802.11b provides a speed of 11 Mbps and operates using the 2.4 GHz frequency.

107. B. The Internet Security Association and Key Management Protocol (ISAKMP) is responsible for negotiating and conducting the key agreement.

108. D. ICMP Type 11 provides the source with a "Time Exceeded" message. Time exceeded is more prevalent if satellite communications are involved and an IP booster is not in use.

109. D. The Lightweight Extensible Authentication Protocol (LEAP) is a Cisco proprietary protocol and can be used in place of TKIP.

110. A. NBT (NetBIOS over TCP/IP) uses UDP 137; NetBIOS session uses TCP 139; NetBIOS datagram uses UDP 138.

111. B. ASLEAP is a vulnerability that takes advantage of the weak password architecture in the LEAP protocol. If there is a requirement to use LEAP, ensure that you implement a very strong and complex password policy.

112. A. The WAP will send out a beacon frame advertising its SSID to wireless devices.

113. C. Implementing user and security awareness training is a cost-effective solution. Not only does it raise awareness in the organization, it is also free to implement.

114. A. Stateful firewall keeps track of all communications and inspects the packets. If a packet is somehow injected into the stream, the firewall will know and will drop it. Although this capability does slow down the network, it provides an extra layer of defense.

115. B. In this scenario, you are conducting gray box testing. Because you are given a network mask to go off on, you now know how big of a network you are testing. Even though this is your only clue, it is still partial knowledge of the environment that you are now operating in.

116. D. The DMZ is a network segment that both private and public network users can access. The DMZ segment gives public Internet users access to resources but doesn't necessarily allow them in the private network. Web and email servers are most commonly used in this type of configuration.

117. B. In a hybrid-mesh topology, a mesh topology is participating in another topology.

118. A. A dual-home firewall is one that has two network interface cards (NICs). The more NICs you have, the more you can segment networks with. In this case, the firewall is managing two different subnets based on the logical diagram.

119. D. The flags portion is missing. The URG, ACK, PSH, RST, SYN, and FIN flags are used in TCP connections.

120. D. Sequence numbers are incremented each time the source sends a packet to the destination. The acknowledgement value is what the receiver can expect next from the sender. To determine the total sequence amount, if the ACK is set to 200 (or whatever value it is determined to be at the time) and a window size is set to 170, the client can expect sequence numbers from 200 to 370. To complete the TCP connection, the final flag is set to ACK.

121. C. A rootkit is a set of tools or applications that can have direct administrator and kernel access to a computer. This poses a significant problem because it is very hard to detect because the kernel or root level is the most secured part of the operating system.

122. A. Passive reconnaissance is the process of actively gathering information and intelligence without directly touching or impacting the target or victim. Most information can be gained through public means such as the daily newspaper.

123. A. In a smurf attack, the adversary spoofs a victim's IP address and then pings the broadcast address. All nodes on that network segment will send back an ICMP echo reply, causing a DoS on the victim's system.

124. B. Shoulder surfing is a passive attack. Simply peering over the shoulder of an unsuspecting person is one of the easiest ways to capture credentials. If the adversary is able to steal the card somehow, the adversary will now have access to the account.

125. D. Whenever a client is trying to establish a Secure Sockets Layer connection, the first packet is flagged to "Don't Fragment." This prevents an adversary from injecting their own packets into the middle of a secure data stream.

Practice Test 4

1. **A.** RSA uses two prime numbers that are factored together and can create a key size up to 4,096 bits. The RSA algorithm can be used for digital signatures and encryption.

2. **B.** In asymmetric encryption, two keys known as the public and private key are mathematically related.

3. **D.** Transport mode provides protection to the payload through encryption. Using tunnel mode provides encryption to protect the message header and the payload.

4. **B.** Request for Comments (RFC) 1918 defines 10.0.0.0–10.255.255.255, 172.16.0.0–172.31.255.255, and 192.168.0.0–192.168.255.255 as private, non-routable IP addresses.

5. **B.** An A record maps an IP address to a hostname. It is the most commonly used DNS record type. A user can alter the host file by inputting an IP address followed by a domain name or hostname.

6. **D.** Because an adversary can create a man-in-the-middle attack using a public router, he can force the user to downgrade to using SSL 3.0. This exploit can work only if the server and the client browser support SSL 3.0.

7. **B.** URL obfuscation is the process of changing a value so it means the same but is in a different format. For example, instead of using http://22.56.98.4, you would convert the IP address to binary, which is 00010110001110000110001000000100. Then to ensure that the value will work properly with the browser, you convert the binary value into decimal format, which is http://372793860. This may allow you to bypass firewall restrictions since a binary rule may not be configured for the firewall.

8. **A.** Social engineering encompasses all the options. It is the process of tricking and manipulating people into, for example, opening spam email, providing account login information over the phone, and tailgating or piggybacking through a mantrap or turnstile. Training employees on social engineering is a cost-effective solution for preventing such incidents.

9. **C.** The 802.11g band provides speeds up to 54 Mbps; however, the more clients connected to the access point, the slower the wireless speed becomes.

10. **D.** RC4 in WEP uses anywhere from 40- to 232-bit keys for encryption. The weakness in WEP is not the encryption itself but rather the initialization vector, which is small. If the adversary can gather enough packets, they can derive the key used for encryption.

11. **B.** MSConfig provides the user with different applications affiliated with Startup, Services, and Boot. Among other things, MSConfig can inform the user what applications currently in startup may have been remotely or covertly installed.

12. **A.** Initialization vectors using WEP are sent in the clear and are not protected by encryption because they are part of the header.

13. **A.** The * symbol is a value that means *everything*. The statement SELECT * FROM Vegetables queries a SQL database to "select everything from the vegetables table." The request being sent to the SQL database will then return all the values listed in the Vegetables table.

14. B. Digital signatures enforce nonrepudiation, providing assurance that the sender of an email is who they say they are.

15. C. The ticket-granting ticket (TGT) is provided to the key distribution center (KDC). If the ticket is legitimate, the KDC will issue a ticket-granting service (TGS) ticket. The subject will then present the ticket-granting service ticket to the server and will be provided with access to the system or resource that was originally requested.

16. D. The term *chain of custody* describes how evidence is transported, handled, and maintained.

17. B. A business continuity plan (BCP) assesses a variety of risks that may impact business operations. As these risks are identified, the business will document solutions to either eliminate or reduce the risks. The customer who tasked you to overlook the BCP is attempting to get an outside unbiased look at its plan and looking for recommendations to improve it.

18. A. Generally, a fraggle attack will use UDP port 7 (echo port) to deliver a DDoS to a victim's computer.

19. A. Spim, or Spam over IM, is a type of spam that includes unsolicited messages sent over an instant messaging application. It can include unwanted advertisements and even Short Message Service (SMS) texts.

20. D. Direct sequence spread spectrum (DSSS) employs all the available frequencies at one time. It provides higher throughput and can allow the recipient to reconstruct data if it is lost or corrupted.

21. B. A hoax is a form of social engineering. The goal is to either trick or manipulate people to act or behave in a certain way. For example, calling in a bomb threat at a bank and then observing how people react is a way of learning their procedures for such an event. The adversary then understands what to look out for with this type of hoax.

22. A. Having a baseline image allows for security administrators to install the minimum security policies and applications for the workstation. Before it goes into production, the workstation will receive the latest security updates and policies.

23. B. Fuzzing is a technique that puts random input values into a system. The purpose of fuzzing is to determine how a program or an application may respond to certain types of input. This can aid in troubleshooting when applications are developed or penetration testing operations are conducted.

24. D. Remote wipe is the technology the owner would use to delete or wipe personal data and information from a mobile device. In this case, using encryption is not an appropriate response because it is designed to protect data. Remote lock does not protect personal data. Remote backup does not prevent personal data from being improperly disclosed.

25. B. The client has been authenticated once it receives its ticket-granting ticket (TGT) and is then considered an authenticated principal in the Kerberos realm. Although the client received the TGT, that does not necessarily mean they have access to all of the resources.

26. C. By targeting the HVAC units, the black hat has the potential to DoS all the systems in the server room. The heat must be raised to a high enough temperature to cause the peripherals to overheat and crash. The heat generated by the servers along with the HVAC temperature being raised will ensure a quick DoS state and minimize the response time of the security administrators.

27. C. Assigning risk is another way to refer to insurance. An organization may use insurance to cover risk that may be too expensive to mitigate, accept, or even ignore.

28. A. Forensics is a scientific approach to collecting evidence. In order for the evidence to be used in court, the chain of custody must not be broken and the evidence must be complete.

29. A. For recovery from an incident to be quick, an incident response plan should be developed and practiced with an organization. The incident response plan outlines how to respond and how to gather information about the adversary in order to develop a case to pursue legal action or even prosecution.

30. B. In 1994, Netscape adopted the SSL security protocol because the demand for Internet security grew.

31. C. Dividing large networks by creating VLANS and subnets makes them more manageable.

32. D. RFC 3227 is *Guidelines for Evidence Collection and Archiving.* It addresses how to approach evidence collection, handling, and archiving. It was published in 2002.

33. A. Privilege escalation occurs often in the work environment. It may not be intentional, but it is a security vulnerability that is a result of not reviewing user profiles and not conducting an exit interview when a user either leaves or is transitioned to another department or role.

34. A. Top Secret is the highest classification used. To be granted this security label, you have to meet a need-to-know requirement.

35. B. DRP is a solution that quickly restores business operations after a disaster event. DRP also employs strategic methods of implementing redundant fault-tolerant systems and procedures.

36. C. The incremental bit is set when the data has been changed since its last backup. If the data was not changed and the bit that flags for an archive was not set, the backup will not occur.

37. D. The MTD is the amount of time a business can be inoperable and still recover. Disaster recovery planning and business continuity planning are designed to prevent a business from exceeding the MTD.

38. D. Humidity between 40 and 60 percent prevents hardware peripherals from becoming too hot to spark and cause a fire and too cold to cause moisture and corrosion.

39. B. An acceptable use policy (AUP) outlines what is deemed acceptable and what is not when accessing the company's information systems. The user must sign a document that signifies their agreement to the terms. If the user agrees and then violates the policy, they may be held liable for damages, which could be grounds for termination.

40. D. If you are conducting an assessment of the disaster recovery plan (DRP), you are currently in the maintenance and assessment of the DRP element. This can include testing the DRP and even training individuals according to the DRP.

41. B. Containment is the most important phase of an incident response procedure. Security administrators should focus on containing malicious activity to prevent data from being corrupted or services from being degraded.

42. C. The original sender receives a SYN/ACK from the receiver signifying the acknowledgment of the SYN packet.

43. A. The Python Advanced Wardialer System, or PAWS, is an application that can be used to war dial ISDN telephones.

44. B. When the RST flag is set, it forces the sender to close their connection as well alerting the receiver on the network to close their connection as well.

45. B. In Snort, any value that has ! in front of it is excluded from the rule. For example, `alert tcp !home_net any - > external_net any` alerts any traffic that is not from the home network that is going out the external network.

46. A. NTSF file steaming allows a user to hide a file behind any other file and makes it invisible in terms of file directory searching.

47. D. In C, gcc is the command to compile the source code, and then it creates the executable file that is used to run the program.

48. D. Dumpster diving is the process of collecting information that an organization carelessly throws away. Some documents contain valuable information, such as bank account statements and even personal identifiable information that should be shredded.

49. C. Tailgating is attempting to blend in with other personnel to enter a secured area. The goal is to trick the security personnel into believing that you are in fact part of the maintenance crew.

50. A. Ransomware is a type of malware that encrypts the operating system. Until the user pays and retrieves the key to decrypt the operating system, they will not have access to their files. In recent years, this has been an increasing threat among users who download files using peer-to-peer applications.

51. A. Server clustering is grouping multiple servers together so they act cooperatively. It provides redundancy, fault tolerance, and improved performance.

52. B. A subject is given a security label called a clearance. Their trustworthiness to process sensitive information determines their level of clearance, such as secret or confidential.

53. C. All safeguards should be considered based on the cost and benefit analysis. The cost and benefit of the safeguard should not exceed the value of the asset that is being safeguarded.

54. A. The absence or weakness of a safeguard causes a vulnerability. If there is a great chance of the vulnerability being exploited, the likelihood of the risk goes up.

55. A. TEMPEST is a U.S. government security program that outlines how to minimize and reduce data being emanated through electromagnetic signals. Materials such as concrete and lead can block receivers from picking up electromagnetic signals that carry data.

56. C. A Faraday cage blocks electromagnetic signals from emanating. It is most often used to protect highly classified data from eavesdropping.

57. A. Secure Copy Protocol (SCP) uses TCP port 22 in conjunction with SSH RCP.

58. B. An extranet is a business-to-business solution whereby businesses have access to each other's resources but not to their local area networks.

59. D. In order for an anomaly IPS to function properly, a network baseline must be determined. It is recommended to determine the baseline during peak hours and low-usage hours.

60. B. In a fraggle attack, the adversary crafts a packet and pings the broadcast address. The result is that all the nodes within the subnet will respond to the address the adversary forges, causing a DDoS on the victim's computer.

61. B. Slowloris is a tool that was designed to target Solaris web servers. It starved the server by creating multiple TCP sockets, which in turn would cause a DoS on the server or its services.

62. B. A threat agent is a subject that acts upon a vulnerability and causes an exploit. For example, a home that does not have a lock on its front door is vulnerable to a burglary. The threat agent is the person who carries out the burglary.

63. A. A cyber persona is a person who is either a regular user or an administrator and has access to an information system.

64. A. Platform as a service is a configuration in which the customer can have access to the operating system and applications. Its purpose is to provide a complete package in a virtual state rather than paying for hardware and the software and housing it locally.

65. C. Shoulder surfing is used when the adversary is attempting to steal personal information. It is commonly used at automated teller machines to pick up a personal identification number.

66. B. IPv6 has IPsec natively built into it. Among other capabilities, IPv6 also uses anycast and eliminates using broadcast.

67. C. Port Address Translation, or PAT, uses the unique IP address to be mapped to a port address as the mechanism for keeping track of web connections. It is also referred to as NAT Overload.

68. B. Classless Inter-Domain Routing (CIDR) is a protocol that allows for networks to be created with different sizes.

69. B. VLANs are separate virtual local networks that can be used to segregate workstations. This practice can be used to group workstations in a "need to know" network and can prevent others from accessing the network through port security.

70. B. ICMP operates at the layer 3 of the OSI model. ICMP uses ping, echo-request, and echo-reply. It is commonly used to diagnose and troubleshoot network connections.

71. B. The best method for making a backup copy of a system is using a bit-level image. Although a full backup is another alternative, it does not fully create a mirror image of a system.

72. A. Although zero day vulnerabilities are difficult to combat, the best alternative is user awareness training. This can include validating the receipt of emails and matching hash values of software being downloaded from a website.

73. C. Botnets are groups of computers that a bot herder or a zombie master controls. The computers do not necessarily have to be physically located near the master; the master can control the bots via IRC or instant messaging services.

74. D. Snipernet uses port 667. It is a backdoor commonly found on Windows 95 and 98.

75. D. Using a Trojan to install a backdoor gives the black hat the ability to covertly access the computer at any time. This allows the black hat to steal information as the victim continues to utilize the system.

76. A. Cain & Abel allows the user to pull passwords from packets from live network captured packets.

77. A. Heartbleed used the protocol extension called Heartbeat. Heartbeat is used to determine the health of a system on the network by providing a status every so often.

78. B. Disabling the CBC mode cipher is another option for preventing the POODLE exploit. The cipher block chaining mode that is used in the Data Encryption Standard is sufficient to defend against POODLE.

79. A. Guards, fences, lighting, bollards, and even environmental design are forms of physical controls that are used to reduce and prevent an adversary from breaching the grounds of a facility.

80. D. Doom, which is a backdoor Trojan, allows a remote connection to the infected host. It was named after the first-person shooter game called Doom, which was developed by id.

81. D. A hub is a layer 1 device that broadcasts all the data on all of its ports. Once the adversary gains access to a port, they do not have to do anything other than collect the data.

82. C. A proxy firewall acts as a middleman between the client and the destination server. It will terminate the connection on behalf of the client and can also facilitate packet filtration and conduct stateful inspection.

83. A. A lightning strike is considered a natural event. Other types of events that can impact assets include human and environmental.

84. C. The DSA is considered a scheme with an appendix, which means that is must have the original message in order to validate and verify the signature.

85. D. In 1978, Ron Rivest, Adi Shamir, and Leonard Adleman proposed using their version of public key cryptography that was far more efficient and more secure than its competitors. Although there were different public key cryptosystems available during that time, they were not as secure as RSA's public key cryptosystem.

86. A. A land attack causes the victim's system to either crash or freeze because it does not know how to respond to an invalid TCP segment.

87. C. The sequence number is the third field in the TCP header. It consists of 32 bits and is used to aid the recipient on packet consolidation and sequencing.

88. A. TCP is a segment that provides reliable transportation for IP datagrams.

89. B. In this scenario, the adversary would need to have the token and the PIN in order to digitally sign the email. Using a multifactor approach increases the security posture. The victim in this scenario may have somehow lost their card along with the PIN and may face adverse actions as a result of not reporting their card lost or stolen.

90. A. Kerberos is an authentication, accounting, and authorization (AAA) server that uses tickets to grant access to resources. Although it is widely used, it has a few drawbacks, such as using symmetric cryptography and being susceptible to man-in-the-middle attacks.

91. D. A stack pointer is pointed at the top of the memory stack. Memory uses the concept of last in, first out (LIFO), and instructions are either pushed onto the stack or popped off of the stack.

92. C. The macro feature that is found in Apache OpenOffice and in Microsoft Office can be used to execute malicious commands. The macro feature is now disabled by default.

93. B. A signature matches characteristics of a virus. If a polymorphic virus has compromised a system, it would change its signature, making it extremely difficult to detect and eradicate each time it is called.

94. A. Physical control is used to restrict physical access to sensitive equipment, a facility, or an area.

95. D. The risk mitigation plan is a formal document. It captures all of the vulnerabilities identified during the assessment with recommended courses of action. It provides information on how to mitigate and reduce vulnerabilities.

96. D. War dialing phone numbers to connect to a modem is a method that is used to gain access to a server. Most servers that still have their modems connected are often overlooked because they are forgotten. These active modems pose a significant threat and should be disabled and unplugged if they are not required for business operations.

97. D. The command useradd followed by the username is the proper way to add a user.

98. A. The find command will locate a specified file based on the name in the current directory tree given by the user. Because of the intense search effort, it can be slow, but nonetheless, it will almost certainly locate the file.

99. B. X.509 certificates can be retrieved by using the Heartbleed bug. In this case, it is recommended to revoke X.509 certificates if there is a chance that they may have been compromised.

100. A. Risks, threats, and vulnerabilities are the three types of assessment that can be used to analyze the current security posture.

101. D. Flood guarding detects flooding and DoS activity and, if tuned properly, reacts in order to disrupt the attack on the network.

102. B. Implicit deny is the default security posture that is set for firewalls. The network administrator must configure the firewall to allow appropriate traffic to enter or leave the network.

103. C. SNMP uses port 161 as the agent and port 162 is used for management.

104. B. The Internet Security Association and Key Management Protocol (ISAKMP) is often referred to as the security association manager. It is primarily responsible for managing the agreed method for authentication between two parties.

105. A. WPA2 Enterprise allows for AAA severs such as RADIUS and TACACS to be used.

106. C. With spoofing, the adversary intends to falsify information, such as changing the source address of a datagram to the address of the victim; therefore making it difficult to trace the adversary's IP address.

107. B. Boinks posed a significant threat before Microsoft was able to address the issue. Beforehand, when packet crafters sent an invalid UDP packet destined for DNS services, it caused the Windows system to crash or freeze.

108. C. Using LDAP injection, the adversary can craft statements if the front-end web server will accept LDAP query statements. It is best practice to ensure that the server performs sanitization on input values.

109. A. Hopping from one part of the file system to another is called traversing the directory. This tactic is often used if conventional methods such as creating a shell session are not possible.

110. B. Heaps are allocated in a dynamic fashion. Unlike stacks, a heap is generated when an application demands more memory than what was allocated.

111. A. One of the best practices in cyber security is to reduce the surface threat; therefore, it is recommended to disable all ports that are not used by the sever.

112. D. Fragmentation, or session splicing, is a method to input data in a SYN packet. SYN packets pad their data payload field. In most cases, firewalls will allow a SYN packet to pass through because a client is trying to initiate a connection.

113. A. Signature identification in Snort is a unique value that represents a particular rule.

114. B. Ferret is a tool that allows a user to capture cookies between systems. Other tools that can facilitate this type of attack are Cain & Abel and Hamster.

115. B. SEASAME (Secure European System for Applications in a Multi-vendor Environment) is an authentication, accounting, and authorization server. A user that is requesting access to a server must be authenticated by the authentication server and then request access to the privilege attribute server.

116. D. This operation is a revoke operation under the Take-Grant model. The subject that has the read and write permissions on an object has removed the read permissions. The subject can now only write to the object.

117. A. The final output to the diagram is the digital signature. This diagram depicts an overview of the RSA digital signature generation.

118. A. During the signature verification process, the message is verified by using the results of the signature that is copied. In this case, the user does not need to have the original message in order to determine the integrity of the message.

119. A. When you're XORing, the values that match. such as 0 and 0 or a 1 and a 1, will XOR to a 0. If the values are mismatched, such as 1 and 0 or 0 and 1, then their XOR value will be a 1.

120. C. A monalphabetic cipher, also known as a replacement cipher, exchanges one character for another to complete the encryption and decryption process.

121. D. The BP, or base pointer, is used to reference the local variables in the memory stack.

122. B. On line 8, the ACK is sent back to 23.253.184.229 and is set to 1. This completes the three-way handshake.

123. A. The flag is 0x02, which is "don't fragment."

124. B. TLS uses key agreement, which cannot be derived by plain text. The adversary must conduct a man-in the-middle attack to retrieve the key.

125. A. The current connection is not vulnerable to Heartbleed because it affects only connections using TLS versions 1.0.1 to 1.0.1f.

Practice Test 5

1. A. Enumeration is the act of identifying specific services that a target machine is running. It involves connecting to the system, gathering login credentials, and finding open ports and even programs that are installed.

2. A. Although a man-in-the-middle attack may be a possible answer, it does require some sort of interaction on a switch, which is not passive. Sniffing is the correct choice and can be done by using a protocol analyzer such as Wireshark.

3. D. Although complex passwords are great to use, a longer password will maximize the key length in the encryption algorithm. In this case, the longer the password, the more secure it is, even if it is a simple password (provided it's not in the dictionary).

4. B. In the directory /var/log, the administrator can access the events that that were previously recorded by the operating system.

5. C. The administrator username that Linux defaults to using is root. Best practice to harden a Linux system is to change the default administrator's login to a username other than root.

6. A. Port Address Translation, or PAT, is the method that maps a single IP address to a port that is unique to a web or Internet connection. One IP address can have many port numbers assigned based on connections.

7. B. The resource identifier (RID) is part of the SID and identifies the user, a domain, or a computer.

8. A. Conducting ping sweeps and enumerating a target allows the pentester or black hat to fingerprint an operating system.

9. B. The time that is returned to the user, based on the hops the packets take, is recorded in milliseconds. It is usually displayed as *ms* in the terminal.

10. C. DES has a key space of 64 bits, but 56 bits is the actual key length it uses; the other 8 bits are for parity use.

11. C. The Rijndael algorithm was selected to replace DES. It was renamed by NIST as the Advanced Encryption Standard (AES).

12. C. The ACK flag is sent to the originator of the connection and signifies the establishment of the TCP three-way handshake.

13. D. A pair of values such as 1 and 0 or 0 and 1 will produce an XOR output of 1.

14. B. The Securely Protect Yourself Against Cyber Trespass Act makes it unlawful for individuals to take over a system and collect PII without permission from the owner.

15. A. Google Dorks is a collection of sites that are found by pentesters, hackers, and script kiddies. It provides a list of sites that may be vulnerable to SQL injection attacks.

16. A. The header fields such as source and destination port numbers along with length and checksum have a field length size of 16 bits.

17. B. The value that declares the second administrator within Windows is identified as a Resource Identifier (RID) with a value of 501. Administrators start with a RID of 500, and the RID is incremented by one for each additional administrator that is created.

18. C. Ping sweeping the subnet will identify what nodes currently reside on the network. Nodes that are off or not within that certain subnet will not respond back with an ICMP echo reply.

19. D. The Domain Name System uses UDP port 53 for querying and zone transfers.

20. A. Cain & Abel is a tool that is developed for Windows. Among other things, such as ARP spoofing, Cain & Abel can be used to crack passwords by using the dictionary method or by brute force.

21. B. The SYN flag initiates the half-open connection. By sending more SYN packets and not responding to the SYN/ACK packets, it is possible to starve the target of its resources, which will cause it to freeze or crash.

22. D. Dig is a tool that is found in Linux systems. It can be used to query information about a server that is hosting DNS services.

23. B. When you use the alert rule type, the administrator will be notified only if Snort matches the rule to the network traffic.

24. D. When you use -sT, Nmap will conduct a full TCP connect scan on a host or even a subnet, if required.

25. C. A firewall is a logical control and is often known as a technical control.

26. B. The / indicates that the current user is located in the root directory when they operating in a Linux environment.

27. A. Impersonation is the act of claiming or pretending to be another valid user. The adversary will most likely try this as an option to gain access to a system because it requires the least amount of effort.

28. D. Driving around to pick up open wireless access points is called wardriving. Tools like Aircrack and Silica can be used to help identify access points.

29. C. ARP poisoning is when the adversary injects their own MAC address in order to sniff traffic on the LAN.

30. B. Windows can receive an input value of up to 127 characters within the field.

31. A. A keylogger, which can be a hardware or software solution, records the input that is generated from the user. Most often, the input that is received is either recorded locally to the device or transmitted back to the owner of the keylogger.

32. D. Using ifconfig in Linux will display wireless adapters and Ethernet devices that are currently installed on the workstation.

33. B. The /bin directory contains the basic commands Linux utilizes.

34. C. Piggybacking is the act of trying to blend in with the crowd in order to circumvent security measures. In this case, the black hat is using boxes to play on the kindness of people to gain easy access to a facility.

35. B. Cookies are text files that contain information about your connection to a web server. They can hold authentication and session details.

36. D. An adversary who records open access points by marking their location on buildings nearby is engaging in war chalking. This signifies to others that there is an open access point to use.

37. B Metamorphic viruses change themselves every time they infect a file. For the most part, metamorphic viruses are difficult to detect with antivirus software because they constantly change their signature.

38. D. SHA-1 was developed by the NSA, and it was soon apparent that it had flaws. In 2005, the US government made an effort to replace it due to its flaws.

39. A. Port 8080 is an alternative to using port 80 for web servers.

40. A. Using -T is considered the paranoid scan, which is the slowest scan possible to evade detection.

41. A. Wireshark is an application that can inspect both wireless and Ethernet packets.

42. B. Web crawling is the process of combing through a website and copying every page. It is resource intensive and, if there is an IPS/IDS in place, may alert security administrators.

43. D. The command passwd followed by the username, which is user, and the password, which is pass123 in this example, will set the password for the account.

44. B. Using arp -a will display the current ARP cache that the workstation is holding.

45. C. Nslookup is an application that provides information about a server that uses DNS. Nslooupk can also show who made the zone transfer and when it occurred.

46. B. Parent domains are designated by .com, .net, .org and even .gov, to name a few. They are also known as top-level domains.

47. D. Scanning and enumeration is the second phase of the hacking methodology, followed by maintaining access and ending with covering your tracks.

48. C. Public key infrastructure, or PKI, uses certificate authorities to sign certificates and issue them to subjects.

49. A. NIST uses http://nvd.nist.gov to publish the latest vulnerabilities for public knowledge.

50. C. Competitive intelligence is the process of using your competitor's information to your advantage. Products that the competitor has on the market may be used for analysis and even reverse engineering.

51. C. SNMPv1 transported community strings as a method of authentication through plain text. Because hackers were able to use SNMPv1 to exploit nodes, it was later upgraded to version 2 and then later version 3 in which the community strings are now encrypted.

52. A. RADIUS is an authentication, authorization, and accounting server that is used to facilitate an enterprise solution for access control. In this case, WPA2 Enterprise will use RADIUS as a means to provide a secure service to its users.

53. B. When separation of duties is enforced, one subject cannot accomplish a specific task without the other. The intent is to prevent collusion and maintain the integrity of that specific task.

54. C. A vulnerability is an absence of countermeasure or defense. If a vulnerability exists, it means that there is a threat that can be exploited.

55. A. In a replay attack, the adversary captures credentials and then uses them at a later time. Although credential harvesting sounds right, it is not the correct answer. Credential harvesting is luring victims through social engineering to capture their credentials to be either used or sold in the black market.

56. D. The client must have the SSID in order to be associated to an access point. Association to an access point is not authentication; the user must have the password to be authenticated to the access point.

57. A. The user must first have a wireless card set to promiscuous mode to sniff wireless packets from the network.

58. D. Using rm as the command will remove a file from the directory. To remove files and folders recursively, the command is rm -r.

59. A. A digital signature on an email is proof that it came from the original sender. Using asymmetric encryption such as Digital Signature Authority (DSA) and RSA are methods to provide nonrepudiation for emails.

60. B. Operational controls, also known as management controls, are policy driven. Users will be granted access based on their position in the organization and their need to know for certain resources.

61. B. A rootkit is a type of malware that will provide the adversary with a backdoor entrance to the compromised system.

62. B. Metasploit is a framework that can be used in many different scenarios to compromise a system and user accounts. It is primarily found in Kali Linux, but it can also be downloaded as well.

63. C. Using net use followed by ipc$ "" /u: "" will set up a null session with your target. It can be used in part with password sniffing efforts.

64. C. Base64 encoding is used to change binary code into the ASCII format. It can be used to circumvent firewalls and IDSs.

65. A. Emails that solicit banking information are classified as spear phishing.

66. A. AirCheck is an application that is employed by Fluke. It allows the user to walk around and locate wireless signals.

67. C. The -T4 switch allows the user to scan a node or a network in a fast manner.

68. A. The URG flag allows for a packet to be sent out of sequence and out of band.

69. B. A /25 indicates that the user is scanning a subnet that hosts 128 nodes.

70. C. The user would most likely be using Google. Some sites list other sites that were found to be vulnerable to SQL injection; in this case, these listed sites are known as Google Dorks.

71. B. The supervisor can force an employee to take a mandatory vacation. This allows the supervisor to see if fraudulent activities still occur.

72. C. Using the public key of the receiver guarantees that the information that the sender submits cannot be open by anyone other than the receiver, who can decrypt it with his private key. This scenario uses the asymmetric method for encryption.

73. B. A PTR record indicates that the IP address is mapped to a hostname. In this case, it is used in a reverse manner that is most often associated with email server records.

74. A. Firewalking is a reconnaissance type of action that determines the point at which a packet is being blocked by a firewall.

75. D. Malware that locks the user from their device and demands payment in exchange for the key is ransomware. It uses cryptographic software to encrypt and prevent the user from accessing their device.

76. D. An auto iris lens will adjust as the daylight condition changes.

77. A. Anything that is publicly available, such as the contents of a newspaper, is consider open-source information.

78. C. Duty rotation is a method used to deter fraudulent activity. It is also used to help cross-train and provide redundancy.

79. A. Increasing the time rate will force the DNS server to update the DNS cache. This will reduce the likelihood of users becoming victims of site redirection attacks and other DNS poisoning activities.

80. A. Using `filetype:` in Google will search for websites that contain the file type. For example, `filetype:pdf` will search for PDF files.

81. B. The SHA-1 algorithm produces an output value of 160 bits.

82. A. The X.509 is the digital certificate standard that is used with certificate authorities.

83. C. Asymmetric encryption uses a public and private key that are mathematically related. No other keys can be used with the two that are related.

84. A. The public key is available on the certificate so users can communicate with the subject in a secure manner.

85. C. The black hat installed a keylogger, which records every key that was pressed on the ATM. The black hat will return at a later time and retrieve the keylogger and download the contents to either use or sell.

86. D. A SYN flag will receive an RST response if the port is closed.

87. A. POP3 uses port 110 for email services.

88. D. CSMA/CD uses a back-off timer to prevent data collisions on an Ethernet network.

89. C. A behavior-based IDS can alert when there is abnormal activity being conducted on the network. In order for the IDS to be effective, a baseline must be set during peak and off-peak times.

90. B. ARP poisoning the default gateway will cause you to receive all the traffic on the network. Proceed with caution, however, because if your workstation does not have enough processing power and there is high network activity, you can potentially cause a DoS on the network.

91. A. Bollards are used to prevent vehicles from ramming into a building. They are usually made of solid steel or reinforced concrete.

92. C. SESAME uses asymmetric encryption as a secured method of authentication. Kerberos provides only symmetric encryption.

93. C. Wireshark can be used to monitor and capture network activity.

94. B. Port 21 is the command port for FTP. This port allows for arbitrary commands to be received from the user.

95. D. Files are not objects that Active Directory utilizes.

96. A. Social Engineering is a tool within Metasploit that allows the user to spoof social media websites and even craft spear phishing emails.

97. A. ADmutate is a tool that can craft scripts and encode to hide its signature from anti-malware engines.

98. A. ICMP Type 3, Code 3 is "destination unreachable, port unreachable," which indicates that the client is down.

99. B. In the OSI model and the TCP/IP model, the Transport layer remains the same.

100. A. The Data-Link layer encapsulates the header and trailer of the packet.

101. B. Traceroute can be used to determine if a firewall appliance is being used.

102. B. A NULL scan will not provide a response if the port is opened on the distant end.

103. A. One method of fingerprinting a machine is to conduct a port sweep on all of the machines ports. This may not be ideal if the user is trying to be sneaky, as this is a loud traffic generating scan.

104. A. The SRV record is used to advertise services based on the hostname and the ports of the server.

105. D. The SYN packet initiates the TCP connection.

106. B. The serial number is a unique value that identifies the certificate that is provided by the certificate authority.

107. C. RSA uses two large numbers that are factored together as its basis for encryption. It is used to create digital signatures and symmetric key exchange.

108. A. A SID of 500 is the first administrator's account. The SID of the account created will increase by 1.

109. B. Covering your tracks is the process of deleting and altering log files and users' names so that that the victim is unable to identify the hacker.

110. B. The /etc/passwd file is used to store administrative information about a user such as their name, phone number, and office number.

111. A. UDP port 137 provides name services with NetBIOS.

112. C. The alert rule type will create a log and alert the administrator if a packet matches the specified rule in Snort.

113. A. Back Orifice is a tool that can be used for remote administration.

114. B. Netstat provides the user with information on what connections are currently active on the client. It also provides the IP address and what state the connection is in, such as listening or established.

115. B. As shown in the bottom of the packet, it is annotated that the flags set are A and F for ACK and FIN, and their value is set using 1.

116. A. The destination port that is used in the current TLS connection is 51738.

117. C. Using Netstat, the computer has an established connection coming from the stackoverflow web server on TCP Port 52017.

118. D. The TTL value is 57.

119. C. In traceroute, an indication that a user encountered a firewall is annotated by the ***. In this example, the firewall occurred at hop 15.

120. C. In the first hop, 192.168.1.1 is the source for the traceroute request.

121. A. The client will receive the server's authentication to be granted access to the requested services. This is the third step in the Kerberos process.

122. A. Raeleah has both read and execute permissions for Object 3 in the access control list.

123. C. In the bottom section of the packet, the value that is displayed in plain text shows that the user is using Mozilla Firefox as their browser.

124. A. The alias record is annotated by the CNAME record type. In this case, `rayojo .tripod.com` is the alias that falls under the `members.tripod.com` zone.

125. A. The SSID that is using the highest channel is Rokugan5.

Index

Comprehensive Online Learning Environment

Register on Sybex.com to gain access to the online interactive test bank to help you study for your CEH certification—included with your purchase of this book! All of the practice tests in this book are included in the online test bank so you can practice in a timed and graded setting.

Go to `http://sybextestbanks.wiley.com` to register and gain access to this study tool.

Do you need more? If you have not already read Sybex's *CEHv9: Certified Ethical Hacker Version 9 Study Guide* by Sean-Philip Oriyano (ISBN: 978-1-119-25224-5) and are not seeing passing grades on these practice tests, this book is an excellent resource to master any CEH topics causing problems. This book maps every official exam objective to the corresponding chapter in the book to help track exam prep objective by objective, challenging review questions in each chapter to prepare for exam day, and online test prep materials with flashcards and additional practice tests.